PEGASUS
Library

Karin v. Maur

The Sound
of Painting

Prestel
Munich · London · New York

Front cover: Josef Albers, *Treble Clef*, 1935,
  detail (see pages 102–103)
Spine: Juan Gris, *The Violin*, 1913, (see page 66)
Frontispiece: Moritz von Schwind,
  Cat Symphony, 1868, (see page 114)

Library of Congress Cataloging-in-Publication
Data is available

Translated from the German by John W. Gabriel,
Worpswede
Copyedited by Philippa Hurd, London

© Prestel Verlag
Munich · London · New York, 1999

© of works illustrated by the artists, their heirs
or assigns, except in the following cases: Josef
Albers, Giacomo Balla, Joseph Beuys, Charles
Blanc, Georges Braque, Pol Bury, Alexander
Calder, Camille Claudel, Fortunato Depero,
Theo van Doesburg, Johannes Itten, Alexei von
Jawlensky, Jasper Johns, Wassily Kandinsky,
Paul Klee, Yves Klein, František Kupka, El
Lissitzky, René Magritte, Armin Martinmüller,
Joan Miró, Francis Picabia, Jean Pougny,
Alexander Rodtschenko, Niki de Saint Phalle,
Arnold Schoenberg, Kurt Schwitters, Gino
Severini, Leopold Survage, Jean Tinguely, Henri
Valensi, Panayotis Vassilakis by VG Bild-Kunst,
Bonn 1999; Salvador Dalí by Demart pro Arte
B.V. / VG Bild-Kunst, Bonn 1999; Marcel
Duchamp by Succession Marcel Duchamp /
VG Bild-Kunst, Bonn 1999; Henri Matisse by
Succession H. Matisse / VG Bild-Kunst, Bonn
1999; Piet Mondrian by Mondrian / Holtzman
Trust, c/o Beeldrecht, Amsterdam, Holland /
VG Bild-Kunst, Bonn 1999; Pablo Picasso by
Succession Picasso / VG Bild-Kunst, Bonn 1999;
Man Ray by Man Ray Trust, Paris / VG Bild-
Kunst, Bonn 1999.

Prestel books are available worldwide.
Please contact your nearest bookseller
or one of the following Presel offices for
information concerning your local distributor:

Prestel Verlag
Mandlstrasse 26 · 80802 Munich
Tel. (089) 381709-0, Fax (089) 381709-35;
16 West 22nd Street · New York, NY 10010
Tel. (212) 627-8199, Fax (212) 627-9866;
4 Bloomsbury Place · London WC1A 2QA
Tel. (0171) 323 5004, Fax (0171) 636 8004

Designed and typeset by WIGEL@xtras.de
Lithography by ReproLine, Munich
Printed and bound by Passavia Druckservice,
Passau

Printed in Germany on acid-free paper

ISBN 3-7913-2082-3

The Sound of Painting　7

Runge's Vision of a Synthesis of Art and Music　10

Wagner and Synesthesia　12

Musical Imagery: Gauguin and Matisse　19

The Painter-Composer Ciurlionis　24

Kandinsky and Schoenberg　30

Harmony and Dissonance　38

"Forms of Time" in Painting　43

The Chromatics of Light and the Rhythm of the Cosmos　46

From Sequential Image to Film Sequence　54

Infusing the Pictorial Space with Musicality and Dynamics　60

Noise Sculpture and Pictorial Choreography　68

Synesthetic Investigations of the Russian Vanguard　78

Music in Colored Light and *Harmonia Mundi*　83

Dance Analogies and "Absolute Rhythm"　94

The Serial Principle and Transformed Material　102

The Intermedia Synthesis　110

Graphic Music　114

Plastic Sound　121

Notes　126

Index　127

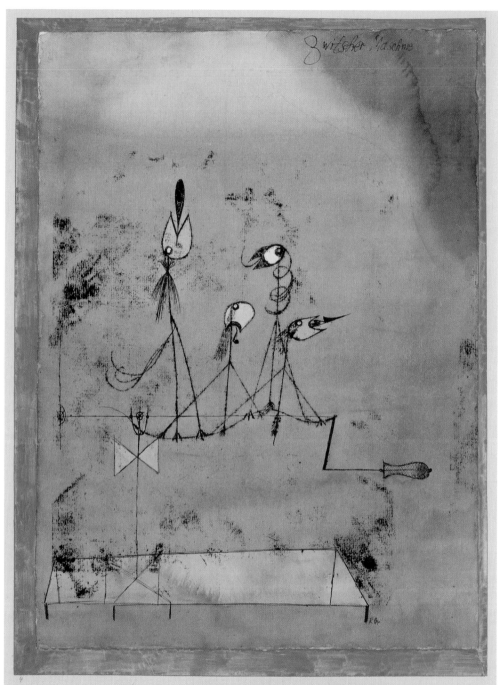

Zwitscher Maschine

4   1922./151   Die Zwitscher-Maschine

The Sound of Painting

Painters have always been intrigued by music, its incorporeality, its sovereign independence of the visible and tangible, and its freedom from the obligation to imitate nature that for centuries was felt to be binding on European art. While poetry, too, despite its higher degree of abstraction, remained tied to the concrete and nameable, music was able to unfold in a free realm delimited only by the rules of tonal harmony derived from its intrinsic means. This radius of action continually expanded in the course of the last century until finally—concurrently with the breakthrough of painting to non-objectivity—even the traditional barriers of tonality were brought down.

Now, as soon as we begin to compare something visible with something invisible, an art that exists in space with an art that exists in time, an imbalance appears, because music, except for its written notation, evades visual perception. Yet we need not go into this semantic dilemma. Let us look instead at actual examples of visual artists for whom music took on the character of a model in many respects and became a key source of innovation. And the influence has been mutual.

Since the end of the last century, music in turn has received key impulses from art. A prime instance is Claude Debussy's seemingly impressionistic technique of "stippled notes" and his suppression of the principle of musical development through time in favor of juxtaposed fields of contrasting tone color which seem as if detached from the temporal flux. Or, later, Igor Stravinsky, who expunged all vagueness and subjective evocation from his compositions to establish, with harshly contrasted complexes of sound, what has been called "a kind of musical Cubism."[1]

Paul Klee (1879–1940)
The Twittering Machine
(*Zwitschermaschine*), 1922
Watercolor, pen and ink over oil drawing,
41.3 × 30.5 cm
The Museum of Modern Art, New York

Composers and painters alike have frequently gleaned new ideas from an approximation to, or borrowings from, procedures used in the sibling art. This reciprocal relationship runs like a continuous thread through the entire century. Music stood behind the birth of pictorial abstraction and the revolutionary unrest in the arts that, in the years before World War I, pervaded the great art centers from Paris to Moscow and Prague, from London to Rome and, finally, New York. This admittedly had been preceded by epoch-making discoveries in physics and chemistry, which radically altered the traditional view of the universe and revealed beneath its visible phenomena a micro- and macro-cosmos of unprecedented scope and mystery. Artists began to sense that their visual language, and a mimetic depiction of visible appearances, were no longer adequate to this emerging new universal scheme. In his autobiography, *Rückblicke* [Retrospections], written in 1913, Wassily Kandinsky recalled that "one of the main obstacles" on the path to abstraction "was swept away by a scientific event. This was the further division of the atom. The disintegration of the atom was, to my mind, analogous to the entire world. Suddenly the thickest walls collapsed. Everything became insecure.... I wouldn't have been surprised if a stone had melted in midair before my eyes and grown invisible...." From this shock Kandinsky drew the conclusion that "for me, the realm of art grew ever more [distinct] from the realm of nature, until I had a complete awareness of both as autonomous realms."[2]

In search of a visual idiom adequate to the new world view, artists turned to music and its independence of material, physical fetters. With music as an ideal, they divorced their imagery from the objective context, thereby liberating colors and forms. Yet in order to avoid falling into mere ornamentation, arbitrariness, or chaos, they knew that the elements of painting must also be composed

how the music + art relationship began.

Paul Klee
Polyphonally Defined White
(*Polyphon gefasstes Weiss*), 1930/140
Watercolor and ink on cardboard,
33.3 × 24.5 cm
Kunstmuseum Bern, Paul-Klee-Stiftung

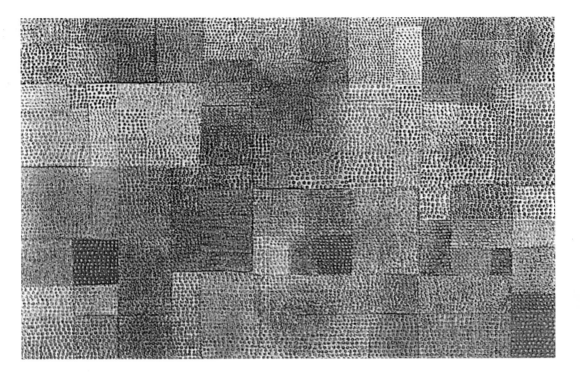

and ordered in a way similar to music. They found
a model, on the one hand, in the new tone language
then being developed in parallel by contempor-
aneous composers, and on the other in the contrapuntally organized structure of polyphony. With
reference to the latter, Paul Klee realized that "in
the eighteenth century music already perceived
and resolved the paths of abstraction, which were
then confounded again by the program music of
the nineteenth. Painting is only beginning this
task today."[3]

Paul Klee
Polyphony (Polyphonie), 1932/273
Oil on canvas, 66.5 × 106 cm
Öffentliche Kunstsammlung,
Kupferstichkabinett, Basel,
E. Hoffmann-Stiftung

Runge's Vision of a Synthesis of Art and Music

Historically, as the tract literature records, the arts have long competed for pre-eminence, with music and painting especially measuring themselves against each other. While in the Renaissance, with Alberti, Leonardo, and Dürer, painting served as the touchstone, thinkers of the Enlightenment advocated a clear distinction among the arts and accorded them equal rank, most notably Lessing in his 1776 critical study *Laocoon, or On the Limits of Painting and Poetry*. The Romantics, in contrast, envisaged breaking down the barriers between the various genres to create a *Gesamtkunstwerk*, a total, comprehensive, or what today would be termed a multimedia or interdisciplinary work of art. In this project, music was granted the leading role, not only by composers and poets but by painters as well. Whether Wackenroder or Tieck, Heine or Runge, they all considered music, "nearest to religion," to be the highest and purest art form, whose immediate effects on mind and soul brought men closest to the wellsprings and workings of Creation. Runge saw in music the common primordial source of all the arts and a guarantor of beauty. "Music, after all," he wrote, "is always that which we call harmony and serenity in all three arts. There must be music through words in a beautiful poem, just as there must be music in a beautiful picture, and in a beautiful building, or in the divers ideas expressed through line."[4]

Long before the rediscovery of Johann Sebastian Bach, which is generally associated with Mendelssohn's Berlin performance of 'The St. Matthew Passion' in 1829, Runge discovered the possibility of composing a figurative painting, his *Lesson of the Nightingale*, on the basis of the fugal principle of imitation. The leitmotif in the central oval field,

Philipp Otto Runge (1777–1810)
Day (Der Tag), 1803/1807
Sheet three of the *Times of Day* cycle,
engraving, 72 × 48 cm
Staatsgalerie Stuttgart, Graphische Sammlung

inspired by Klopstock's ode 'Die Lehrstunde,' shows Psyche teaching Amor how to play the flute. This motif is repeated, in a *grisaille* imitation of bas relief, in three variations around the margin, "ever more abstract and more symbolic the farther removed they are from the picture." In a letter to his brother Daniel of 4 August 1802, Runge explained that the picture had become "the same thing as a fugue is in music. It has brought me to the realization that this sort of thing happens just as much in our own art, namely, how relieved one feels when one has written down the musical movement that lies in a composition as a whole and lets variations of it shine through the whole again and again."[5]

F U G E

During the same period, in connection with his sequence *Times of Day* cycle, Runge oriented himself to the symphonic form and its movements. The drawings and prints devoted to Morning, Midday, Evening, and Night simultaneously symbolized the seasons of the year, in the context of the story of Creation and the eternal cycle of genesis and decay. Runge envisaged the painted version, which was never finished, "as an abstract, painterly, fantastic, and musical poem with choirs...a composition for all three of the arts in one, for which the art of architecture should erect a building all its own."[6]

Philipp Otto Runge
Night (Die Nacht), 1803/1807
Sheet four of the *Times of Day* cycle,
engraving, 72 × 48 cm
Staatsgalerie Stuttgart, Graphische Sammlung

Half a century later Runge's vision of a work of
art encompassing painting, music, poetry, and
architecture experienced a mythical sublimation,
in Wagner's musical dramas. His grandiose amal-
gamation of the arts set off a wave of synesthetic
enthusiasm. It was augmented in France, in the
wake of a scandal caused by a *Tannhäuser* performance, by Baudelaire's defence of Wagner and
the formulation of his theory of *correspondances*.
Writing in the *Revue Européenne* for April 1861,
the poet stated, "it would truly be surprising if a
musical tone could not elicit a color, if colors could
not evoke a melodic motif, and if notes and colors
were not suited to conveying thoughts; especially
since these things have been expressed by means of
mutual analogy from time immemorial, ever since
the day God created the world as a complex and
indivisible totality."[7] And as if this were not enough,
Baudelaire then quoted the first two strophes of
his poem *Correspondances*, anthologized four
years previously in *Les Fleurs du Mal*, whose final
verses invoke this primordial unity of the Genesis:
"As long reverberations flow afar into / a dark and
deep oneness majestic as / the night and endless as
day's brilliance, so cor- / respond the perfumes of
colors and tones."[8] In Wagner, in whom he had
interested himself long before the Paris performance, Baudelaire found in the field of music a
complete confirmation of his theory of synesthetic
correspondences, a "universal analogy" that rested
on the covert affinity of all the senses.

Wagner was also crucial for the artist Henri Fantin-
Latour, a great admirer of Baudelaire. His experience
of the first Ring cycle, performed in Bayreuth in
August 1876, led to a profound change of outlook.
Fantin-Latour's sophisticated realism metamorphosed into a mystically tinged symbolism that
culminated in allegorical Wagner fantasies on the

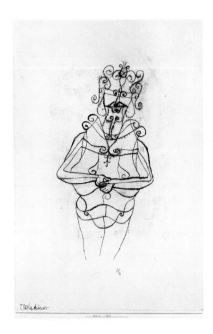

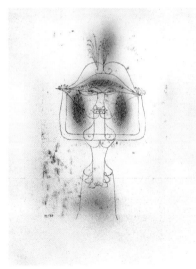

Paul Klee (1879–1940)
Tannhäuser, 1924/197
47 × 30.8 cm
Philadelphia Museum of Art,
The Louis E. Stern Collection

Paul Klee
Singer at the Comic Opera
(*Die Sängerin der komischen Oper*), 1925/225
Lithograph and watercolor on wove,
60.7 × 46 cm
Ulmer Museum, Ulm

Twilight of the Gods, The Rhine Gold, Parsifal, and *Lohengrin.*

The Wagnerism of the day led, in 1885, to the founding of the *Revue Wagnérienne*, for which Mallarmé wrote a prose text that oscillated between fascination and disavowal, "Richard Wagner— Rêverie d'un poète français." In France it triggered a strong tendency towards a unification of the arts on the basis of synesthesia. This was manifested not only in scientific research into synesthetic phenomena such as the hearing of colors, but in the multisensory program of Paul Fort's *Théâtre d'Art* and Lugné-Poe's *Théâtre de l'Œuvre*, in the journal *La Revue Blanche*, the poetry of Rimbaud and Verlaine, the novels of Huysmans and Maeterlinck, and above all in the synthetist painting of Paul Gauguin and the Nabis. Victor Segalen, at the conclusion of his article on "Synethesias and Symbolism," quoted a passage in a letter from his friend, the poet Saint-Pol-Roux: "Supreme art in literature can only be achieved through an alliance of all the senses, controlled by sensibility and spirit.... Art has become complete, *synthetic, symphonic.*"[9]

In the 1890s, the musical element in painting often went hand in hand with an allegorical symbolism. In Gustav Klimt's preciously sensitive painting of 1895, *Music*, a sphinx stands for the ineffable nature of music. In the dream visions of Odilon Redon, such as his lithograph of 1894, *The Celestial Art,*—a title meant both literally and figuratively—the etherial, metaphysical character of music and its divine origins are evoked (see page 14).

The Wagner cult and the overwhelming experience of his music had a liberating effect on artists, shifting their attention from allegory and metaphor to the expression of musical moods through form and color. Where the great symphonic composers Beethoven and Brahms were involved, a greater emphasis on content came to the fore. Max Klinger, in his etching sequence *Brahms Fantasies* of 1894, and Klimt in his *Beethoven Frieze* of 1902, were both inspired to project cosmologies evoking the destiny of humankind. Klimt even translated the hymn from Beethoven's Ninth, "Freude schöner Götterfunken—Diesen Kuss der ganzen Welt," almost literally into visual allegory. Yet the image was saved from mawkishness by introducing linear interweaves with fluctuating rhythms, creating an interplay of empty spaces with groups of figures, and placing the angels' choir in a statuesque sequence, all evoking the dynamics of the crescendo that culminates in the final hymn.

With certain fin-de-siècle artists, this thematic and literary emphasis began to make way for an atmospheric mood elicited by the intrinsic effects of pictorial means. A prime case in point is James McNeill Whistler, an American artist who was active in London and Paris. Already in the early 1860s Whistler began to attune his figure paintings to certain color chords and give them musical titles such as *Symphony No. 1.* His nocturnal views of the Thames or the lagoon of Venice, such as *Nocturne: Blue and Silver—Chelsea* of 1871, or *Nocturne: Blue and Gold—Old Battersea Bridge,* of 1872–77 (see page 16), in turn inspired Claude Debussy to compose his *3 Nocturnes* of 1897–99. Here Debussy set out to exploit the sound range of an instrumental color, for instance of strings, in analogy to the artist's use of gradations of a single color, principally blue. What Whistler achieved through opalescent nuances of a primary color and vague suggestions of objects, Debussy—in the wake of Wagner—strove to achieve through a scintillating painting in sound. Later, reflections on the surface of water, waves breaking on the shore, or fleeting cloud formations as depicted in Japanese art, such as

"Suggestive art is above all the exciting art of music, in this case even more free and brilliant; [my art] is this, too, through a combination of different, reconciled elements, transmuted and transposed forms which, though without relation to accidental conditions, nevertheless have their logic.... My drawings inspire, but they do not define or determine anything. As in music, they transport us into the ambiguous realm of the indeterminate."

(Redon, *An Artist's Creed*, 1898)

Odilon Redon (1840–1916)
The Celestial Art (*L'art céleste*), 1894
Lithograph, 31.5 × 25.8 cm
Kunstmuseum Winterthur

Jean Theodore Fantin-Latour (1836–1904)
Rhinegold – First Scene
(*L'Or du Rhin – Première Scène*), 1888
Oil on canvas, 116.5 × 79 cm
Hamburger Kunsthalle

"The beginning of Rhinegold with orchestra—muffled murmuring of water, the curtain rises ... and at first nothing is visible, then a greenish glow, then gradually waves can be made out, then rocks, then the water grows luminous, shapes move, women advance and recede, singing. This is unique in its charm, and its music."

(Fantin-Latour to Scholderer, Bayreuth, August 30, 1976)

Hokusai's famous woodblock print *The Great Wave of Kawazawa*, would inspire Debussy in 1903–05 to his symphonic sketch, *The Sea*.[10] Through emerging and dissolving open forms the composer evoked a synesthetic, simultaneous impression of surging ground swell, oceanic breadth, and the effects of changing illumination on the water surface.

James McNeill Whistler (1834–1903)
Nocturne: Blue and Gold – Old Battersea Bridge,
1872–77
Oil on canvas, 68.3 × 51.2 cm
Tate Gallery, London

Max Klinger (1857–1920)
Six Designs for the Print Cycle Brahms Fantasy
(*Brahms Phantasie*), *Opus XII*,
Leipzig, 1894; executed 1888–93
Pen and ink with wash,
approx. 32.5 × 42 cm (sheet)
Staats- und Universitätsbibliothek, Hamburg

Possibly intended as a study for a larger-scale wall decoration.
In 1898 Klimt painted a second, considerably larger version as a
supraporte for the music room in the residence of Nikolaus Dumbas,
a Viennese industrialist (destroyed by fire, 1945).

Inspired by ancient Greek vase paintings, Klimt used the attributes
of kithara and vines to symbolize the Apollonian and Dionysian
principles. A similar female figure with lyre reappeared in his
Beethoven Frieze of 1902, this time as a allegory of "Poetry."

Gustav Klimt (1862–1918)
Music (*Die Musik*), 1895
Oil on canvas, 37 × 44.5 cm
Bayerische Staatsgemäldesammlungen,
Neue Pinakothek, Munich

Musical Imagery: Gauguin and Matisse

It was not his delicate sfumato and the nuance-rich monochromy of his motifs, but their flatness and contouring that helped Paul Gauguin overcome symbolism and accentuate the "musical" suggestiveness of colors and lines. "Think too of the musical role, which color will now begin to play in modern painting. Color, which is just as much oscillating waves as in music, is capable of expressing the most universal and thus the most vague thing there is in Nature: its intrinsic force," he wrote in 1899 to the critic André Fontainas.[11] When five years later, after his first Tahiti journey, Gauguin portrayed the Swedish cellist Fritz Schneklud and gave him his own facial features, he dispensed with symbolic accouterments and restricted himself to a comprehensive, objective, and concentrated design. This augments the metaphorical character of the figure, the impression of a musician listening with his inner ear, as well as heightening the effect of the subdued color chord. The shimmering reddish-brown of the cello, echoed in hair and beard, against the black of the suit, embedded in the darker brown of the interior and contrapuntally relieved by the delicately hued blossoms at the upper left, convey in the medium of painting the sonorous volume of the instrument's sound. For as the artist said: "Everything in my work is calculated and long considered. This is music, if you please! Through arrangements of lines and colors, under the pretext of some theme from life or nature, I arrive at symphonies and harmonies that evince nothing absolutely real in the usual sense of the word and express no ideas, but are meant to provoke thought, like music ... simply through mysterious affinities between our brains and such arrangements of lines and colors."[12]

This was the point of departure for Matisse. Though he remained true to the figure throughout his career,

Paul Gauguin (1848–1903)
The Musician Schneklud
(*U paûpa Schneklud*), 1894
Oil on canvas, 92.5 × 73.5 cm
The Baltimore Museum of Art,
Donation of Hilde Blaustein
in Memory of Jakob Blaustein

even when reduced to pure sign or clothed in melodious contour, Matisse nevertheless managed to pull all the stops of the autonomous language of color and pictorial organization. Music preoccupied him from the start. For years Matisse used to practice on the violin for an hour every day before going to the easel, and in 1917 he depicted himself in this role, in *Violin Player at the Window*.

The violin becomes a musical metaphor when it lies in its open case on a chair, as in the Copenhagen interior of 1917–18, and even when, in other pictures, only its empty case suggests the presence of an invisible violinist. As we know from his American student, Max Weber, there was a mechanical harmonium in Matisse's atelier that played classical music from perforated rolls.[13] Perhaps it was the very same instrument he had already depicted in 1900, in the unusual *Interior with Harmonium*. In 1916, with *The Piano Lesson*, Matisse transposed the *Well-Tempered Piano* and all the exercises necessary to master it into a brilliantly counterpointed composition of fugue-like stringency.

Matisse repeatedly addressed the theme of music, all the way down to a superb formulation in the painting *Music* of 1939. Yet his monumental mural of the same title, painted in 1909–10 for the Russian collector Sergei Shchukin as a companion piece to his famous *The Dance*, was never surpassed in terms of symbolic cogency (see pages 22–23). While the five ecstatically moving nude figures of adolescent girls in *The Dance* float above the azure blue ground like a swirling garland, embodying an elemental joy in life, the five nude boys, playing and singing, are distributed individually and frontally like a rising and falling sequence of musical notes across the green plane, suggesting magical absorption in an archaic shepherd's melody. Both paintings are built on

Henri Matisse (1869–1954)
Interior with Harmonium, 1900
Oil on cardboard, 73 × 55.5 cm
Musée Matisse, Nice

a contrasting triad of the basic colors red, green, and blue, and reflect the way colorism, in Matisse's hands, unfolds an intrinsic force comparable to that of a musical chord. "Colors are forces—as in music," he later explained.[14]

Matisse, though he never entirely abandoned the figurative context, brought to full fruition what Delacroix had called "the musical part of painting" and what van Gogh had predicted for art: "Painting... promises to become more subtle —more music and less sculpture—in short, what will come is color."[15] And in contrast to Cézanne, who valued balanced chromatics and stated that artists should "modulate instead of modelling,"[16] Matisse in 1907 began juxtaposing large, flat planes of color and playing their contrasts off against each other.

Henri Matisse
Dance, 1909–10
Oil on canvas, 260 × 391 cm
The Hermitage, St. Petersburg

Opposite page:
Henri Matisse
Music, 1910
Oil on canvas, 260 × 398 cm
The Hermitage, St. Petersburg

Mikalojus Konstantinas Ciurlionis (1875–1911)
Sonata No. 5 (Ocean Sonata), 1908
Allegro, Andante, Finale
Tempera on paper, each 73 × 63 cm
State Ciurlionis Museum, Kaunas, Lithuania

The Painter-Composer Ciurlionis

The cosmic visions of the Lithuanian painter–composer Mikalojus Konstantinas Ciurlionis still bore an affinity with Symbolism, and his usually multipartite picture sequences followed certain structural principles of music. In his *Fugue* (see page 26) of 1907, for instance, the rhythmical succession of rows of sharply pointed trees and their reflections in the water illustrate the principles of inversion and close harmony in polyphonal composition. The diaphanously inter-woven, multiple layering of the Allegro movement in his *Star Sonata*, dating from the same year, features a soaring, hyperbolically curved, cone-section form around which play the pulsating rhythms of alternating light and dark bands. Multiple dimensions of planes in space are

brought into simultaneity on the surface, as if cinematically projected one over the other, to evoke the fluctuating interweave of a musical time–space continuum.

Ciurlionis, who died in 1911 at the age of only thirty-six, left behind not only a considerable œuvre of musical compositions—symphonic poems, choir and piano music, primarily sonatas, preludes, nocturnes and fugues, in which a kind of serial tone sequence was already employed—he also produced a body of painting comprising about three hundred tempera works and prints, all executed in the brief period of 1903 to 1909 and now in the Ciurlionis Museum at Kaunas, the Lithuanian capital. As a practitioner of the two sister arts he relied on a theosophical conception, according to which music and painting represent symbolic reflections, in the Pythagorean sense, of the divine order, which can be seen with the aid of the "spiritual eye" and heard with the aid of the "spiritual ear."

In both fields Ciurlionis relied on an instinctively sensed geometry to establish correspondences between the music of the spheres, "musica mundana," and the music of men, "musica humana."[17] Shortly before his death the belated delivery of an invitation from Kandinsky prevented him from participating in the second exhibition of the New Artists Association of Munich [Neue Künstlervereinigung München] in autumn 1910.[18]

It is not known how Kandinsky's attention was drawn to Ciurlionis. Although his works were exhibited from 1908 onwards in Vilnius and Kaunas, St. Petersburg and Moscow, and in 1910 in Paris, Kandinsky could not have seen them, since he was in Munich and Murnau at the time. Yet through his intensive contacts with the Russian art scene and his compatriots living in Munich—such as the composer Thomas von Hartmann and the artist Marianne von Werefkin—Kandinsky would have heard of the nine-year-younger Lithuanian and his phenomenal dual talent, and seen reproductions of his works in art journals, prompting him to invite Ciurlionis to participate in his group's show.

For Ciurlionis the unity of the arts was not the goal but the point of departure of his creative activity. "There are no dividing walls between the arts," he declared. "Music combines within itself poetry and painting, and has its own architecture."[19] Concentrating in his musical compositions especially on the principle of the fugue, Ciurlionis transferred the polyphonal structures of music to painting through a multiple overlay of lineatures and through symbolic motifs. Kandinsky, by contrast, recognized on the basis of his synesthetic experiences that colors and forms could have an

Mikalojus Konstantinas Ciurlionis
Fugue
From the diptych *Prelude and Fugue*, 1907
Tempera on paper, 62.3 × 72.7 cm
State Ciurlionis Museum,
Kaunas, Lithuania

intrinsic effect, independent of objects, and that like the tones in music they were capable of engendering reverberations in the mind and soul of the viewer. Yet both artists were influenced by the esoteric emphases of Symbolism, by its search for the absolute, a metaphysical realm hidden behind appearances which it was the task of art to render visible. And both shared in common a tendency to the cosmological, to phantasmagorias and fables. Though the Lithuanian artist continued to rely on symbolically stylized impressions of nature, in his multiple-movement cycles of paintings he generally employed musical, largely symphonic formal structures. The Russian a short time later entirely sloughed off mimetic fetters, and recast color and line into elemental flecks and vectors, a kind of visual notation that could be employed in a way analogous to musical tones.

Augusto Giacometti (1877–1947)
Chromatic Fantasy, 1914
Oil on canvas, 100 × 100 cm
Kunsthaus Zurich

Wassily Kandinsky (1866–1944)
Impression III (Concert), 1911
Oil on canvas, 77.5 × 100 cm
Städtische Galerie im Lenbachhaus,
Munich

Kandinsky and Schoenberg

"And color, which itself provides a material for counterpoint and contains infinite possibilities, will in combination with drawing lead to the great painterly counterpoint, on the basis of which painting, too, will attain to composition and place itself, as a truly pure art, in the service of the divine."

(Kandinsky, *On the Spiritual in Art*, 1912)

Arnold Schoenberg, before 1911, with the opening sequence of his 2nd string quartet, 4th movement, and his dedication to Kandinsky: "Dear Mr. Kandinsky, I am forever floating in music—and, at last, am relieved of one of my obligations which I would have liked to have fulfilled some time ago." 12.12.1911 Arnold Schoenberg, Städtische Galerie im Lenbachhaus, Munich

Synesthesia was a central concern of the fin-de-siècle Symbolists, and as with Baudelaire and his theory of *correspondances*, the Wagner cult greatly influenced their art. This holds for Kandinsky as well, whose synesthetic experiences, triggered by Wagner's music, encouraged him to devote himself to painting. In his autobiography, *Rückblicke*, the artist described a sunset over Moscow in glowing colors and musical metaphors, saying it reminded him of Wagner's *Lohengrin*. "*Lohengrin* seemed to me to be a perfect realization of this Moscow," Kandinsky wrote. "The violins, the deep bass tones, and especially the wind instruments embodied the entire force of the early evening hour for me back then. I saw all my colors in my mind, they appeared before my eyes. Wild, almost mad lines drew themselves in front of me. I did not dare to state in so many words that Wagner had painted 'my hour' in music. But it became absolutely clear to me that art in general was much more powerful than I had thought, and that, on the other hand, painting was capable of developing powers akin to those of music."[20]

Kandinsky, who was convinced that colors could be heard and himself possessed this gift in high degree, believed that colors directly "touched the soul." By analogy with a piano, he explained that "color is the key, the eye is the hammer, the soul is the piano with its many strings." So intrigued was Kandinsky by analogies between the hues of the spectrum and tone colors that he attempted to place them in a systematic order. He associated primary and secondary colors with certain instruments, yellow with the sound of a trumpet or fanfare, orange with that of the viola or a "warm alto voice," red with the tuba or kettle drum, violet with the bassoon, blue with the cello (an instrument Kandinsky himself played), contrabass, or organ,

Wassily Kandinsky
Fugue (Controlled Impression)
(*Fuga [Beherrschte Impression]*), 1914
Oil on canvas, 129.5 × 129.5 cm
The Solomon R. Guggenheim Museum,
New York

and green with the "sustained, meditative tones of the violin."[22]

A crucial impulse for Kandinsky's plunge into abstraction came from a meeting with Arnold Schoenberg. Schoenberg's music made him realize that the concept of tonal harmony was undergoing a radical change, and that dissonance was becoming a means of expression on a par with consonance. On New Year's Day, 1911, Kandinsky, Franz Marc, Alexei von Javlensky, Marianne von Werefkin, and Gabriele Münter attended a Schoenberg concert at which his two string quartets Op. 10 of 1907–08 and *Three Pieces* Op.11 of 1909 were performed. The second string quartet marked the beginning of Schoenberg's atonal period, for in its fourth movement, as the composer himself explained, "the overwhelming variety of dissonant sounds could no longer be counterbalanced by an occasional insertion of tonal chords."[23]

This concert came as a revelation to Kandinsky's friends and fellow members of the Neue Künstlervereinigung group, because it showed that music had achieved revolutionary changes of very much the kind they envisioned in art. As Franz Marc wrote to August Macke after the concert: "A musical event in Munich has given me a strong jolt—a chamber music soirée by Arnold Schoenberg [Vienna]…. The audience behaved like hoi polloi…. Can you imagine a music in which tonality (i.e., the holding of a certain key) has been completely abolished? I continually had to think of Kandinsky's great composition, which likewise admits no trace of key, and also of Kandinsky's 'leaping flecks' as I was listening to this music, which lets every note struck stand for itself (like white canvas between the color flecks!) Schoenberg proceeds on the assumption that the concepts of consonance and dissonance do not even exist. A so-called dissonance is merely

"A so-called dissonance is only a consonance with greater intervals. This idea concerns me continually while working nowadays, and I apply it to painting thus: It is by no means necessary to let the complementary colors appear next to one another, as in a prism; on the contrary, you can 'disperse' them as far apart as you want. The partial dissonances this leads to are resolved again in the overall appearance of the picture, and take on a consonant (harmonious) effect, in so far as they are complementary in terms of dispersal and degree of saturation."

(Letter of Marc to August Macke, February 14, 1911)

Franz Marc (1880–1916)
Playing Forms (*Spielende Formen*), 1914
Oil on canvas, 56.5 × 170 cm
Museum Folkwang, Essen

consonance
dissonance.

Franz Marc
Sonatina for Violin and Piano
(*Sonatine für Geige und Klavier*), 1913
Watercolor, 10 × 15 cm
Postcard to Lilly Klee, December 1913
Private collection, Bern

a consonance with larger intervals.... Schoenberg, like the Association, is convinced of the irresistible dissolution of the laws of European art and harmony."[24]

The concert prompted Kandinsky to begin corresponding with the composer whom he had not yet personally met. On 28 January 1911 he wrote to Schoenberg: "In your works you have put into practice something I have greatly longed for in music, if only in a vague form. The independent passage through individual adventures, the intrinsic life of the individual parts in your compositions is precisely what I too am attempting to find in the field of painting.... I do believe that the harmony of today is not to be found by the 'geometric' approach (Cubism), but by a decidedly anti-geometric, anti-logical one. And this approach is that of 'dissonances

August Macke (1887–1914)
Colored Composition I (*Homage to J.S. Bach*)
(*Farbige Komposition I [Hommage an J.S. Bach]*),
1912
Oil on cardboard, 101 × 82 cm
Wilhelm-Hack-Museum, Ludwigshafen

"What makes music so mysteriously lovely also has an enchanting
effect in painting. But it takes superhuman power to bring colors
into a system like musical notes. Colors do contain counterpoint,
treble and bass clef, major and minor, just like music. An incredibly
fine sensibility can lend them order without recognizing all of this."

(Macke, 1907)

in art,' that is, in painting to the same extent as in music. And the painterly and musical dissonance of 'today' is nothing else than the consonance of 'tomorrow'."[25]

The experience of the Munich concert flowed directly into Kandinsky's painting *Impression 3 (Concert)*(see pages 28-29), which reflected his impressions on hearing atonal music. The large black area in the upper part of the picture evidently refers to the grand piano on which the *Three Pieces* Op. 11 were played. The dominant basic yellow evokes an expanding motion which, like a strident trumpet note, can be raised to an excruciating force and pitch that enable it to carry great distances. The black, in contrast, is "like a dead void after the extinguishment of the sun, like a profound silence.... It is, in musical terms, a full, concluding rest.... This is outwardly the least sounding of colors, over which every other color, even those with the weakest ring, sound stronger and more precise."[26]

It was not until a letter of 6 February 1911 that Kandinsky came to mention Schoenberg's own paintings. He was so impressed by them that he invited the composer to participate in the first exhibition of the Blauer Reiter. Interestingly, Kandinsky preferred not so much the *Visions*, ecstatic dreamlike apparitions with incandescent eyes or hands groping into emptiness, as the self-portraits and portraits, in which Kandinsky found confirmation of Schoenberg's theory of "great realism" as opposed to his own theory of "great abstraction." As he explained in an essay on the composer's painting published in 1912: "The picture is an outward expression of an inward impression in painterly form.... We see that, in each of Schoenberg's paintings, the artist's inward desire speaks in a form that suits it. Just as in his music ... Schoenberg dispenses in his painting

In the "most recent period my works have very small formats, but the imagery is even more profound and spiritual, speaking solely through color. Since I had felt that I would not be able to work in future due to my illness, I am working like a man obsessed on my little 'Meditations.' And now I leave these small, but to me significant works to the future, for people who love art."

(Javlensky, *Memoirs*, 1970)

Alexei von Javlensky (1864–1941)
Fugue in Blue and Red
(*Fuge in Blau und Rot*), 1936
Large Meditation XXIII, No. 20/V
Oil on paper, mounted on cardboard,
25 × 17.7 cm
Collection of Maria Javlensky, Locarno

with the superfluous (i.e., the harmful) and goes by a direct path to the essential (i.e., the necessary). He leaves all 'improvements' and fine painting unnoticed by the wayside.... The term I should most like to apply to Schoenberg's painting is sheer painting [Nurmalerei]." Schoenberg himself did not attach any particular significance to his depictions of people and landscapes, considering them more in the nature of exercises. The *Visions* were more important to him, because —as Kandinsky had recognized—they served to "give expression to emotions that find no musical form."[27]

Arnold Schoenberg (1874–1951)
Funeral of Gustav Mahler
(*Begräbnis Gustav Mahler*)
Oil on canvas, 43 × 30.5 cm
Collection of Lisa Jalowetz Aronson, New York

"Schoenberg's paintings fall into two categories: the first are people and landscapes painted direct from life; the second, intuitively sensed heads, which he calls 'Visions.'

Schoenberg himself describes the former as necessary finger exercises.... The latter (as much as the former) are painted to give expression to emotions that find no musical form.... In the first place, we *immediately* see that Schoenberg paints not in order to paint a 'pretty,' 'charming,' etc. picture, but that he really does not think of the picture at all in the course of painting. Regardless of the objective result, he seeks *only* ... the means which appear inevitable to him at the moment.... The painting is an external expression of an internal impression in pictorial form.... If we measure Schoenberg's works in painting by the yardstick mentioned, we immediately see that what we have here is *painting*, whether it stands 'on the sidelines' of the great 'contemporary' movement or not....

His *Self-Portrait* is painted with what is known as 'palette mud.' What other colored material could he have chosen to achieve this strong, straightforward, concise impression? ... One Vision is *merely* a head on a very small canvas (or a piece of cardboard packaging). *Only* the red-rimmed eyes speak out strongly."

(W. Kandinsky, in *Arnold Schönberg*, Munich, 1912, p. 59 ff.)

Arnold Schoenberg
The Red Gaze (*Der rote Blick*), 1910
Oil on cardboard, 32.2 × 24.6 cm
Städtische Galerie im Lenbachhaus, Munich.
Loan of Mrs. Nuria Nono

Harmony and Dissonance

Artists began to grow ever more aware of the fact that colors, like musical notes, possess their own, intrinsic tone quality, and that, quite apart from their use as local colors, they could be employed by analogy with the rules of musical harmony to release their full, intrinsic power. This recognition of the musical character of color led, in the first decade of the century, to a more or less radical divorce from the objective context, accompanied by an increasing study of color–tone correspondences with an eye to arriving at coloristic principles analogous to those of the musical theory of harmony. A pioneer in this field was Adolf Hölzel, who in 1904 declared: "I think that just as there is counterpoint and the theory of harmony in music, there must be a striving in painting towards a definite theory concerning aesthetic contrasts of every type and their harmonious balance.... In this way, that sovereignty with respect to nature could be achieved which raises art to something extraordinary."[28] Hölzel, who was also an excellent violinist, accordingly proceeded to develop a comprehensive theory of composition based on Goethe's and Runge's investigations, but also on those of Helmholtz and Bezold. This theory would subsequently be expanded by his student, Johannes Itten, to eventually become a cornerstone of instruction at the Bauhaus.

Unlike Hölzel, who after his *Composition in Red* of 1905 composed his paintings in largely abstract terms, but often reintroduced objective references after the fact, Kandinsky attacked the white canvas much more directly, and uncompromisingly pared down suggestions of objects to the point of vague rudiments. As a result his imagery, despite its actually having been carefully planned in preparatory studies, has a more anarchic and also a more expressive character than Hölzel's.

"People should read Delacroix's journals more, for instance the conversation with Chopin: Mastering the fugue means nothing more than knowing the element of all reason and all logic in music.... Art is not what the layman thinks it is, namely a sort of inspiration that comes from who knows where, shoots into the blue, and represents only the picturesque surface of things. It is reason itself, which, revealing itself through genius takes a preordained path and is kept in bounds by higher laws...."

"What is harmony other than a combination of opposites conforming to feeling, and its balancing to a certain extent based on certain laws.

The subject of an art work is not productive of harmony. For the image in the musical sense, which emerges solely through the development and processing of autonomous, basic elements, and possesses the highest value of an absolute work of art, the subject is not a necessity."

(Hölzel)

Adolf Hölzel (1853–1934)
Fugue (on a Resurrection Theme)
(*Fuge [Über ein Auferstehungsthema]*), 1916
Oil on canvas, 84 × 67 cm
Landesmuseum für Kunst- und
Kulturgeschichte Oldenburg

The crucial difference probably did not lie in their different temperaments, but in the fact that Hölzel's understanding of harmony was oriented towards classical music, whereas Kandinsky early on grasped the significance of the idea of dissonance. While Hölzel viewed perfect harmony in terms of an equilibrium of contrasts, Kandinsky, spurred on by Schoenberg's music, realized that the conception of harmony was not immutable but was subject to change, a change that brought the emancipation of dissonance (or what had previously been defined as such). Now dissonance was no longer merely tolerated in a neutralizing combination with consonance but was raised to a means of expression on a par with it.

The insight that music was going through a change
quite as epoch-making as that which was emerging
in art became the signal for Kandinsky and Marc
to leave the Neue Künstlervereinigung München
and form a new group, Der Blaue Reiter. They were
convinced that the veritable reinvention of art they
envisaged could be achieved only by overcoming
the borderlines between the genres and searching
for common roots, in a word, through a "unification
of all artistic means and powers." What both the
artists and the composers of the day shared was
a sense of new frontiers to be conquered, and
the aim of renewing art by liberating it from the
fetters of traditional laws of harmony, whether
visual or aural.

Thus the first decade of our century came to witness
almost simultaneous revolutions in music and art.
As Schoenberg was liberating composers from the
system of tempered tonality, the painters were in
the process of jettisoning the system of mimesis
and a unified spatial perspective. Both systems
had been legitimated for centuries by masterpiece
after overwhelming masterpiece, and had become
canonized to the point that they were considered
irrevocable—absolutely essential elements of each
respective art. This explains the anarchic energy that
had to be mustered in order to confront the over-
powering force of tradition with a radical, liberating
act; and it also explains the "atonal" character of
Kandinsky's prewar paintings, which reflect this
process.

Unlike those artists who oriented themselves to
classical music, especially to Bach and Mozart,
Kandinsky—accelerated through his contacts with
contemporary musicians—developed a painting
approach that corresponded to the new atonal
scale (not in the sense of a cause-and-effect relationship, but in that of a confirmation of a path
already embarked upon).

Johannes Itten (1888–1967)
Bluish-Green Sound (*Blaugrüner Klang*), 1917
Oil on canvas, 144 × 91 cm
Kunsthalle Bremen

Just a few years later, though, Kandinsky would begin to temper this style by developing new principles relating to the analysis of abstract pictorial elements, just as Schoenberg would temper his compositions by means of the serial, twelve-tone technique.

František Kupka (1871–1957)
Piano Keys/Lake (Touches du piano), 1909
Oil on canvas, 79 × 72 cm
Národní Gallery, Prague

"Forms of Time" in Painting

The well-known yet nonetheless continually astonishing phenomenon of the nearly concurrent yet mutually independent emergence of abstraction in the great European centers, from Paris to Moscow and Prague, from London to Rome, and immediately thereafter in the United States, may well have been due partly to the fact that artists everywhere had taken their cue from music. They did so not only because of the principles of harmony or color-sound correspondences, but above all because of a factor related to the non-material character of music—its temporality. The search for a "fourth dimension," a hidden force behind visible phenomena, had of course long been underway before Einstein, in 1905, defined this invisible fourth dimension of space as the time dimension in his 'Special Theory of Relativity'. Thus music, which lends shape to time, develops through time, and diminishes with the temporal flux, was "looked upon with envy"[29] by visual artists who felt increasingly constricted by the spatial character of art and yearned to find some way to integrate the missing dimension into their medium. In music, a space-time continuum already existed, since it engendered a continually changing "tone-space." Painting as previously practiced could do no more than evoke three dimensions and capture a certain moment or state; it was considered static, incapable of representing motion except in terms of certain, fixed phases. Natural scientific, mathematical, physical, and philosophical investigations and currents, not least Bergson's *élan vital*, tended towards a withdrawal from the visible world and an exploration of the reciprocal effects of space and time.[30] This led to an increasing urge on the part of artists to expand the limits of their medium, and the most obvious way to begin was to test the categories of the temporal art par excellence for their applicability to visual art.

The disintegration of the unified pictorial space, the fragmentation of the object, the autocratic employment of liberated motif elements, the autonomy of color, form, and line, and the increasing dynamism of all three—these developments, which took place between 1908 and 1914 in the guise of Cubism, Futurism, Orphism, Vorticism, or Synchronism—were basically directed towards opening visual art to the dimension of time. Never before in the numerous programs and manifestos of the avant-garde did there appear so many temporal concepts, such as rhythm, dynamics, speed, and simultaneity, or musical terms such as cadence, dissonance, polyphony, etc., proving the existence of a close link between the temporalization tendencies in art and the reception of musical phenomena.

Marsden Hartley (1877–1943)
Musical Theme No. 2 – Bach,
Préludes et fugues, 1912
Oil on canvas, mounted on masonite,
60.9 × 50.8 cm
Thyssen-Bornemisza Collection, Madrid

Marsden Hartley
Musical Theme, 1912
Oil on canvas, 64.7 × 52 cm
Private collection

"I'm working on a new subject—have you ever heard of anyone trying to paint music—or the equivalent of sound in color—I'm sure you've heard of singers talking about the colors of sounds.... Well, I'm working on this, and there are some artists who tell me that my work must be unique.... There is only one artist in Europe who is working on this and he is a pure theoretician ...—whereas I work utterly intuitively and subconsciously."

(Hartley to Norma Berger, December 30, 1912)

The Chromatics of Light and the Rhythm of the Cosmos

The Czech artist František (Frank) Kupka was perhaps the first to attempt to represent "the kinetic
dimension in painting."[31] Coming from the orbit
of Symbolism, he was profoundly involved in synesthetic sensations and theosophical ideas. By way
of motion studies of dancers (or of his daughter
playing with a ball) and intensive investigations
into color, Kupka embarked on the path to abstraction at an early date. Around 1910, he arrived at
a type of sequential image articulated in terms
of chromatic color progressions, which already
possessed a kinetic aspect.

"By using a form in various dimensions and arrang-
ing it according to rhythmical considerations, I will
achieve a 'symphony' which develops in space as a
symphony does in time," wrote Kupka during this
period.[32] After a series of attempts there finally
emerged, in 1912, a monumental composition,
Amorpha—Fugue in Two Colors, in which musical
movement is condensed into a grand, symbolic
configuration. Based on the principle of polyphony
and fugal variation Kupka lets two voices or parts,
in red and blue, appear in succession, in interweaves, divergences and inversions, thus creating
a "fugue in colors" whose vital, metaphorical motion
evokes an image of the rhythms that inform the
universe.

Musical themes can be traced in Kupka's work
through the late 1930s. They exhibit two tendencies
that are significant for musically inspired painting
as a whole. On the one hand, there are flowing,
cosmically circling motifs that recall floral arrangements, as in *Warm Chromatics*; on the other,
there are constructively built, serially articulated
compositions, some of the earlier of which recall

František Kupka
Fugue in Two Colors (Amorpha)
(*Fugue à deux couleurs*), 1912
Oil on canvas, 211 × 220 cm
Národní Gallery, Prague

Morgan Russell (1886–1953)
Four-Part Synchromy, No. 7, 1914–15
Oil on canvas, 39.4 × 29.2 cm
Whitney Museum of American Art, New York.
Gift of the Artist in Memory of
Gertrude V. Whitney, 1951

"In order to solve the problem of a new painterly structure, we have considered light as tightly linked chromatic waves and devoted closer study to the harmonic combinations among the colors. These 'color rhythms' lend a painting a temporal dimension; they create the illusion of the painting developing over a period of time, like a piece of music ..."

(Russell, in the catalogue to the Synchromist exhibition, Paris, 1913)

Stanton MacDonald-Wright (1890–1973)
Creation Synchromy, 1914
Oil on canvas, 91.3 × 76.5 cm
Hirshhorn Museum and Sculpture Garden,
Smithsonian Institution, Washington, D.C.

"To this point mankind has sought to satisfy its need for spiritual
nourishment only through music.... Yet painting is just as capable
as music of conveying the greatest delight and sense of happiness.
By liberating ourselves from certain obstacles and inhibitions, ... we
have wrest from nature the secrets necessary to bring painting
to this supreme degree of intensity."

(Russell and MacDonald-Wright, Munich, 1913)

The Chromatics of Light and the Rhythm of the Cosmos   49

František Kupka
The Cathedral (La Cathédrale), 1913
Oil on canvas, 180 × 150 cm
Private collection, Washington, D.C.

50

keyboards, such as *Piano Keys/Lake* of 1909 (see page 42), or *Cathedral* (1913), which was inspired by the "dizzying chromatic musicality" of Gothic stained-glass windows[33] and whose vertical sequencing reflects fugal principles in another way.

At about the same period as Kupka in Czechoslovakia, Robert Delaunay in France occupied himself in the wake of Cézanne and Seurat with the relationships between light and color, with a musical sense of time, and with simultaneous perception. From these studies Delaunay derived his theory of "simultaneity," which would have a far-reaching influence both on the German artists of the Blaue Reiter and on the American avant-garde under the leadership of the "Synchromists" Morgan Russell and Stanton Macdonald-Wright. In canvases such as *Four-Part Synchromy* by Russell and *Creation Synchromy* by Macdonald-Wright, (see pages 48–49),as well as in their investigations into color–sound analogies, the two Americans drew their conclusions from Futurism and Orphism. At the same time their paintings showed astonishing affinities with the work of Adolf Hölzel and Johannes Itten, which was based on similar researches, though no direct influence can be posited. On the occasion of their first solo show in 1913 at the Munich Neuer Kunstsalon, the two founders of Synchromism announced that to date only music had been capable of communicating the highest spiritual sensations, but that painting now—after having daringly overcome its obstacles to penetrate into the realm of the unknown—had wrest Nature's secrets from her and heightened them to the utmost intensity. Moreover, they added, painting was closer to reality than music, because visual perception was more intimately linked with Nature than aural perception.[34]

Delaunay, too, considered not music but painting the superior art, if for a different reason. He justified

The painted inscriptions around the colored vowel sequence A-E-I-O-U were taken from Arthur Rimbaud's description of vowel-color links in his 1873 poem 'Une saison en enfer' ('A Season in Hell'). Here Rimbaud makes reference to his famous poem 'Les voyelles' ('The Vowels') of 1871.

Robert Delaunay (1885–1941)
Deliriums II – Alchemy of the Word
(*Delires II – Alchimie du verbe*), 1914
Watercolor, 24.9 × 31 cm
Bibliothèque National,
Cabinet des Estampes, Paris

Opposite page:
Sonia Delaunay (1885–1970)
*Prose of the Trans-Siberian and
Little St. Joan of France*, 1913
Free-verse text by Blaise Cendrars,
"simultaneous colors" by Sonia Delaunay
Folded booklet, 199.5 × 35.5 cm
Editiond's des Hommes Nouveaux, Paris 1913
Musée Rath, Geneva

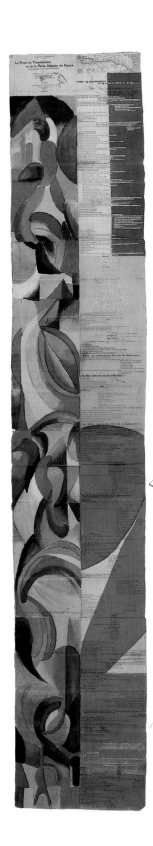

this opinion by reference to the principle of simultaneity: "The movement of hearing is successive, a kind of mechanism; its law is the time of mechanical clocks.... The eye is our most highly developed sense; it is most closely linked with our brain, our consciousness. It conveys the idea of the vital motion of the universe, and this motion means simultaneity."[35]

Based on Seurat's researches, Delaunay employed complimentary color contrasts to release the dynamic effects of color and elicit a sense of optical motion. His insight into the factor of proportionality in color contrasts led him to speak of light as the ordering force in life, the foundation of harmony and rhythm. "Simultaneity in light means the harmony and rhythm in colors, which engender human vision."[36] Apollinaire, proceed-ing from this point, arrived at the concept of "Orphism," which he defined thus in a 1913 article entitled "Modern Painting": "If a simple color determines its opposite color, Delaunay believed that in the case of certain color combinations all the colors of the spectrum would be generated as well. This stylistic tendency can be called Orphism."[37] In Delaunay's *Window Pictures* of 1912, the vision of a merger of light and color, proportion and rhythm, time and motion took on the concrete shape of pure colorforms. These marked the achievement of that purity and musicality in painting whose realization Apollinaire had predicted in 1912, in his essay "On the Beginnings of Cubism": "This art will have so many links with music as only an art that is the opposite of music can have. This will be pure painting."[38]

The determining effect not only of simultaneous contrasts as "synchromous action," but of the temporal principle as a sequential development of the rhythmic dynamism of colors, is seen in *Windows on the City* of 1912. Comprising five conjoined window motifs, this composition marked the first appearance of the overlong format in Delaunay's work. In this case still horizontal, in the 1930s, the period of the *Endless Rhythms*, it would be used in vertical form.

Thus we find consecutive motion—which Delaunay basically rejected—entering and even determining the image after all, because the progressive flux of time is almost imperatively evoked here by an added juxtaposition of forms on the plane. The scroll-like horizontal format of the *Windows*, across which an excerpt from the rhythmical continuum of simultaneous color contrasts extends, greatly impressed the artists of the Blauer Reiter, who visited Delaunay in Paris in 1912. Paul Klee recognized the intrinsic link in these works between the representation of a musical time lapse and the extreme format. As he noted in his diary for 1917: "Delaunay has attempted to shift the accent in art to the temporal, based on the example of the

The 'Window' paintings by Delaunay inspired Apollinaire to write his famous poem 'Les Fenêtres,' which was first published in 1913, in the catalogue to the Delaunay exhibition at the Sturm gallery, Berlin.

Robert Delaunay
Windows on the City
(*Les Fenêtres sur la ville*), 1912
Oil on canvas, 53 × 207 cm
Museum Folkwang, Essen

Paul Klee
Fugue in Red (Fuge in Rot), 1921/69
Watercolor on paper, 24.3 × 37.2 cm
Private collection, Switzerland

"The musician and Bach player Klee, who discovered ever-new formal stimuli in the fugue, also created a group of paintings and colored drawings whose formal structure rests on the principle of imitation or contrapuntal polyphony. In the fugue, as everyone knows, the same theme is taken at various pitches through all the voices or parts, whereby every point in the higher melody corresponds to a point in the lower one. The parts begin one after another, and the theme can be altered, e.g., reversed. In other words, themè, intertwining, polyphony, logic....

Already in its title, the *Fugue in Red* is related to the 'speculative phenomenon' of music. In the four main shapes (jug, kidney, circle and rectangle) we might see theme, reply, theme in the third, and reply in the fourth part. The changing pitch would then lie in the changing character of the forms, the development of the theme in the development of color (yellowish pink – pink – violet). A logical gradation of color plays itself out in logically interrelated shapes...."

(Will Grohmann, *Paul Klee*, 1954)

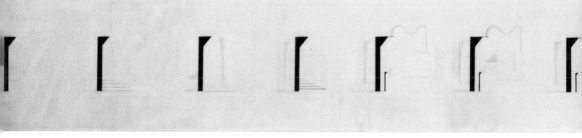

Helmuth Viking Eggeling (1890–1925)
Horizontal-Vertical–Orchestra I
(Fair or *Symphony)*
(*Horizontal-Vertikal–Orchester I*
[*-Messe* bzw. *-Symphonie]*), 1919–21
Pencil on paper, 51.5 × 363.5 cm
First, second and third movements
Kunstmuseum Basel,
Emanuel-Hoffmann-Stiftung

Hans Richter (1888–1976)
Fugue 23 (Fuge 23), 1923/76
Silk-screen print, 61 × 333.5 cm
Collection of Marion von Hofacker,
Irschenhausen

fugue, by choosing a format so long it cannot be taken in at a glance."[39] Klee himself found another solution to the problem in 1920 his *Fugue in Red*, instead of using additive sequences he articulated the plane by means of a layering suggestive of depth and a progressive, prismatic color gradation of the separate motifs (see page 55).

Delaunay's wife, the Russian painter Sonia Terck, created in 1913 an almost two-meter-long, accordion-folded book, based on Blaise Cendrars's free-verse text, *Prose of the Trans-Siberian and Little St. Joan of France* (see page 53). The abrupt syntax of the text, printed in ten different type faces and distributed rhythmically over the whole length of the publication, and accentuated by Sonia Delaunay's interpenetrating "simultaneous colors," evoked the rotating rhythms of train travel on the Trans-Siberian Railway. A simultaneity of colors, letters,

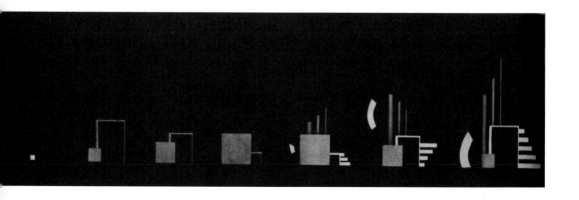

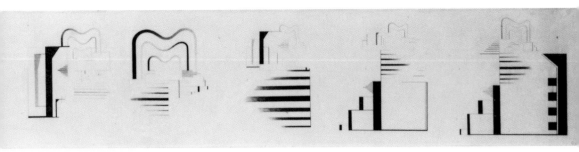

and theme, of sequential motion and simultaneous perception had been achieved, prompting Apollinaire to note in 1914: "Blaise Cendrars and Madame Delaunay-Terck have realized a first attempt at written simultaneity in which the color contrasts incite the eye to read the entire ensemble of the poem in a single glance, just as a conductor takes in the accumulated notes of a score at one glance, or as one perceives at a glance the pictorial and printed symbols of a poster."[40] Certain passages of Cendrars's text are underlaid with blue, yellow, green, and red color fields that suggest relationships between linguistic sounds and certain color qualities. Robert Delaunay would subsequently, in 1914, produce a simultaneous visual translation in watercolor of the famous line from Arthur Rimbaud's *A Time in Hell*: "I invented the colors of the vowels!—A black, E white, I red, O blue, U green."[41] (See page 52).

"The rhythm of a work is identical with the idea of the whole. Rhythm is that which conveys ideas, that which runs through the whole: its meaning = principle, from which each individual work derives its significance. Rhythm is not a definitive, regular sequence of time and space; it is the unity which ties all the parts into a whole."

(Hans Richter, 1971)

Hans Richter
Rhythm 23 (Rhythmus 23), 1923
Scroll painting, oil on canvas, 71 × 427 cm
Collection of Marion von Hofacker,
Irschenhausen

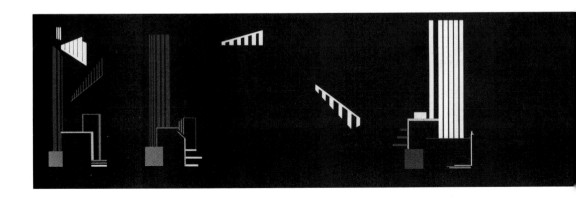

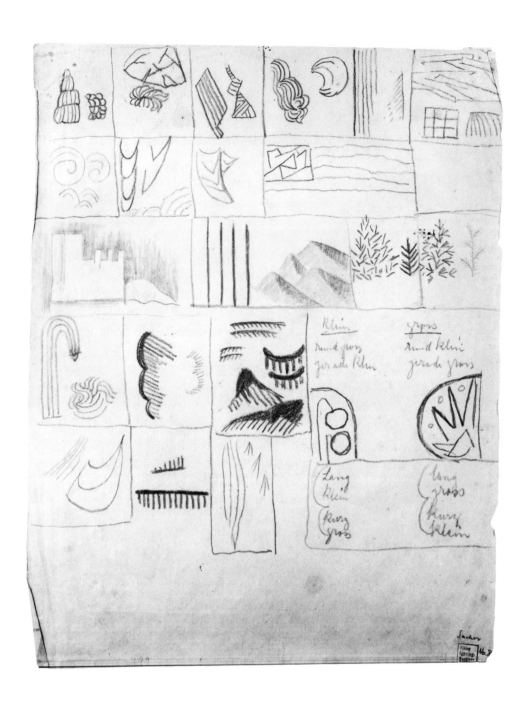

Helmuth Viking Eggeling
Abstract Form Studies, Demarcations with Lines
(*Abstrakte Form-Studien, Begrenzungen mit*
Linien), 1918–19
Pencil, red and blue colored pencil on paper,
30.7 × 23.3 cm, with notes in artist's own hand
Kunstmuseum Basel, Depositum Sacher

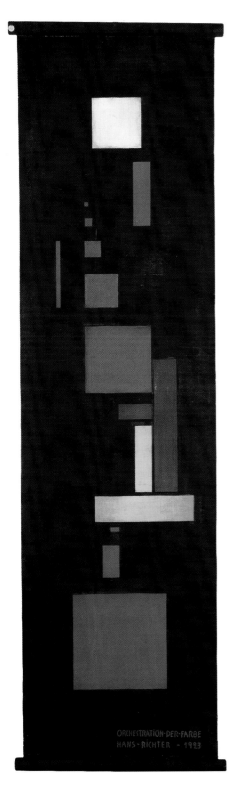

ORCHESTRATION·DER·FARBE
HANS·RICHTER · 1923

The scroll format, inspired in part by the cinematographic studies of E.J. Marey and Eadweard Muybridge, was later employed in many works concerned with a systematic visualization of musical pieces, such as the painted film reels of Viking Eggeling and Hans Richter, or Klee's 1921 transcription of the opening bars of the adagio from Bach's *6th Sonata for Violin and Harpsichord* in G. Klee entered the pitch and duration of the notes in a system of horizontal lines marked by vertical measures, and attempted to visualize tone quality and dynamics by varying the thickness and emphasis of the lines (see page 117).

Similar attempts to transpose musical compositions into art were again made in the 1950s, by artists such as Robert Strübin or Jakob Weder, and also by Luigi Veronesi and Jack Ox, who despite the use of eccentrically long formats usually did not get beyond the transcription of a few bars because, in this regard, painting quite literally runs up against its limits (see pages 118–119).

"In order to methodically play through the possibilities of the color scale as I did in the form scale in 1919–21, I built up an Orchestration of Color in complementaries, contrasts and analogies, a kind of Magna Charta for color. *Orchestration of Color* (in scroll form) helped me as a model and theme for a further 'Rhythm' film (the final one), *Rhythm 25*."

(Richter, 1965)

Hans Richter
Orchestration of Color
(*Orchestration der Farbe*), 1923
Oil on canvas, 153 × 41.7 cm
Staatsgalerie Stuttgart

Georges Braque (1882–1963)
Violin and Poster (*Violon et affiche*)
(Mozart/Kubelick) [sic], 1912
Oil on canvas, 47 × 61 cm
Private collection, Basel

Infusing the Pictorial Space with Musicality and Dynamics

After the Cubists' disintegration of the pictorial space and fragmentation of objects had integrated the process of perception into the image and engendered something in the nature of "temporal forms," which their contemporaries identified with the concept of polyphony, painting itself became a type of instrument. As has recently been noted with respect to George Braque: "Addressing his relationship to music, not only in the scores but as played by certain instruments, at the same time meant ... treating his relationship to painting accordingly. Just as a sequence of notes is not heard independently

of the instrument producing them or the composition to which they belong, a [visual] sign does not disclose itself without its specific hue, configuration, or material character—it cannot be abstracted from the context in which it is inscribed, or better, in which it is 'scored'."[42]

Jean Laude refers here to the instrumentalization of painting, begun by the Cubists and inspired by the musical instrument as motif, which directly affected pictorial design and engendered a dematerialization, motion, and temporality analogous to music (or at least their visual, aesthetic equivalents). The compositions of Braque with their musical references (*Homage to J. S. Bach* or *Bach Aria*) and the paintings of the Puteaux group (Marcel Duchamp's

Georges Braque
Hommage à Bach, 1912
Oil on canvas, 54 × 73 cm
Collection Caroll and Conrad Janis, New York

Sonata of 1911) indicate how the pictorial space and its liberated motif elements are set in vibration, appear to float, glide, and fluctuate.

What gave rise to this musical impression was initially probably a quite general sense of a moment in time made visible, probings and palpitations that released the object-space relationship from stasis and set it in virtual motion. The resulting multilayered interweave of objective and spatial structures was compared with the multiple parts of a musical score, and especially with the polyphony of Bach. "Picasso's paintings truly expand into edifices of Bachian polyphony," enthused the Czech art historian and collector Vincenc Kramář in his 1921 book on Cubism. A year previously Paul Erich Küppers, director of the Kestner-Gesellschaft, Hanover, had extolled the link between this painting style and the structure of Bach's fugues:

Georges Braque
Still Life BACH (Nature morte BACH), 1912
Charcoal and collage with wood-grain paper,
62.3 × 48.3 cm
Kunstmuseum Basel, Kupferstichkabinett,
Gift of Dr. h.c. Raoul la Roche

Opposite page:
Georges Braque
Bach Aria (Aria de Bach), 1913
Collage with wood-grain paper,
black construction paper, charcoal and
white crayon, 62 × 46 cm
National Gallery, Washington, D.C.
The inscription probably refers to Bach's
Aria variata A minor for piano (BWV 989).

Aria de Bach

G Braque

Group portrait of the artist's mother and three sisters playing music (Suzanne seated, Yvonne at the piano, and Madeleine with violin).

"Duchamp plays with the formal possibilities of translating chamber music into visual analogies of rhythmic accentuation and silence within the composition's melodic fabric.... A painting is inself a form of sonata...."

(Lawrence Steefel, 1960; quoted in Arturo Schwarz, *The Complete Works of Marcel Duchamp*, 1969)

The still lifes with instruments of 1912, which marked the transition to Synthetic Cubism, were introduced by the violin melody of the chanson 'O Manon ma jolie! Mon coeur te dit bonjour.' This was the song Picasso associated with his love for Eva Gouel, which he proclaimed in picture after picture with the refrain "Ma Jolie."

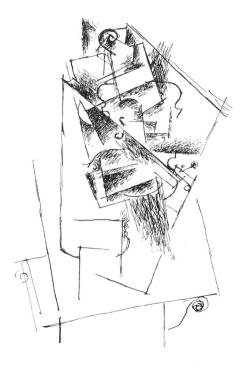

Marcel Duchamp (1887–1968)
Sonata, 1911
Oil on canvas, 145 × 113 cm
Philadelphia Museum of Art, The Louise and Walter Arensberg Collection

Pablo Picasso
Study for a Construction with Guitar Player, 1912
Pen and ink on paper, 21.2 × 13.3 cm
Collection of Marina Picasso
Galerie Krugier, Geneva

Pablo Picasso (1881–1973)
Violin "Jolie Eva" (Violon "Jolie Eva"), 1912
Oil on canvas, 60 × 81 cm
Staatsgalerie Stuttgart

The way music appears through paintings.

"Out of pale harmonies of color, lines arise, prisms protrude, grow out towards us, leap back, chisel steps into infinite space, lead upwards and into the depths, expand, multiply, combine into chords, are suffused with rhythm and begin to dance in the absolute music of space. One experiences this transcendental dynamism in a way no different from the metaphysical counterpoint of Bach's fugues...."[43]

And Daniel-Henry Kahnweiler, who, probably to prevent misunderstandings, had avoided musical comparisons in his 1920 book *The Road to Cubism*, used them lavishly in his later monograph on Juan Gris. "Gris's works recall ... the grandiose musical architectures of Johann Sebastian Bach," wrote Kahnweiler in his chapter titled "Polyphony",

Infusing the Pictorial Space with Musicality and Dynamics   65

Pablo Picasso
Still Life on a Piano, 1910–11
Oil on canvas, 50 × 130 cm
Berggruen Collection, Berlin

Juan Gris (1887–1927)
The Violin, 1913
Oil on canvas, 91.4 × 54 cm
Philadelphia Museum of Art

and added: "When I use the term 'polyphony' to describe the structure of Gris's works of this period, I am convinced it means more than a catchword. Anyone who looks at his 'architectures' ... can easily recognize 'independent voices'. Thus Gris's method can doubtless be termed 'contrapuntal'."[44] Moreover, it is striking how often Braque, Picasso, and Gris included the names of composers, particularly Bach, Mozart, and Debussy, in their paintings and collages.

handwritten note:
* contrapuntal
- interweaving
- lots of different ideas at the same time

* polyphony
- many different voices.

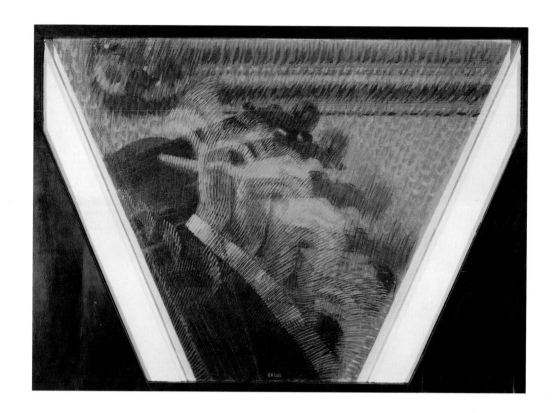

Noise Sculpture and Pictorial Choreography

Giacomo Balla (1871–1958)
The Violinist's Hand (Violinist's Rhythms)
(*La mano del violinista – Ritmi del violinista*), 1912
Oil on canvas, 53 × 75 cm
Collection of Mr. and Mrs. Estorick, London

If the Cubists, at least Picasso, Braque and Gris, largely confined themselves to the neutral theme of still life, the Futurists explicitly addressed motifs of motion. Their concept of simultaneity aimed to capture the multisensory impressions and dynamism of the big city. Since the ear was involved as much as the eye, they had a predilection for motifs that signified noise and speed, whether trains steaming out of stations, automobiles racing down dark streets with headlights blazing, or turbulent mass demonstrations. In the treatment of their animistic imaginations the Futurists took key tips from the time–motion photographs of Antonio G. Bragaglia. A good example is Balla's *Hand of the Violinist* with its repetitive sequencing and translucent color, simultaneously evocative of a space-time and an acoustic process. With the "multiple-phase" image[45] the Futurists introduced a new form of temporality into painting, similar to though apparently independent of that conceived by Duchamp in his famous *Nude Descending a Staircase* of 1912. In 1913 they moved more in the direction of evoking aural phenomena, or "dramatic vibrations"—in other words oscillations of tiered color.

The tendency to an evocation of dynamism often went hand in hand with musical analogies. This is illustrated in an exemplary way by the astonishing development of Luigi Russolo. In 1911 he painted a programmatic picture titled *Music*, which was still quite beholden to Symbolism. An ecstatic vision rendered in forceful colors, it shows the vaguely silhouetted figure of a man playing the piano, from whose keys a melodic line rises in a broad, blue serpentine. Behind the musician's head emerge circular rings whose hues run the gamut from light to dark blue, visualizations of sound waves that fill the whole pictorial space. From its edges, colored beings with joyful or grotesque masks shoot like meteors towards the pianist. According to the artist, these figures symbolize the feelings engendered by music, embodied in the various facial expressions.[46] The complementary color contrasts of the faces combine into visual

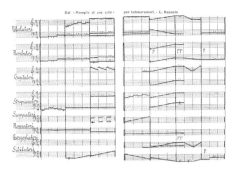

Luigi Russolo (1885–1947)
Score for "The Awakening of a Town," taken from *The Art of Noise* (*L'Arte dei Rumori*), Milan, Edizioni Futuriste de "Poesia," 1916
Private collection, Stuttgart

Illustration from The Art of Noise, 1916
The wood and metal instruments may be classified in six groups:
a) Buzzers (Ronzatore), 80 × 85 × 89 cm
b) Graters (Stropicciatore), 69 × 90 × 120 cm
c) Roarers (Frusciatore), 70 × 105 × 55 cm
d) Hissers (Sibilatore), 55 × 120 × 40 cm
e) Cracklers (Crepitatore), 150 × 65 × 65 cm
f) Howlers (Ululatore), 105 × 80 × 80 cm
The noise instruments were reconstructed by Fred K. Prieberg in 1977 for the Hessischer Rundfunk (Hesse Radio), Frankfurt/Main

"Just as we have attributed, and still attribute, to the human sense of vision the recognition of chromatic vibrations of optical origin, so must we accept the scientific axiom that states that chromatic vibrations produced by sound exist in the atmosphere and are perceptible by the sense of sight; both are effects of a force which can take influence on the atmosphere and hence on the human mind.... Since I have always spoken of vibrations and it is a matter of atmospheric dynamics, I have hopefully succeeded in making clear that the vibrations produced by a force have, as their equivalent, not one color but a number of colors, since we also know that the atmosphere is composed of seven colors and that vibrations are a resolution of the atmosphere."

(Prampolini, *Chromophony: The Colors of Tones*, manifesto, 1913)

Umberto Boccioni (1882–1916)
[The Noise of] the Street Enters the House
(*La Strada entra nella casa*), 1911
Oil on canvas, 100 × 100 cm
Sprengel-Museum, Hanover

Opposite page:
Luigi Russolo (1885–1947)
Music (*La Musica*), 1911
Oil on canvas, 220 × 140 cm
Collection of Mr. and Mrs. Estorick, London

"The predominant impression of the picture: When you open a window, all the noise of the street, the motion and physical presence of the things outside suddenly enter the room. The painter ... brings into the picture everything you would be able to see looking around in every direction from an open balcony."

(Catalogue note in *Die Futuristen*, Berlin, Galerie Der Sturm, 1912)

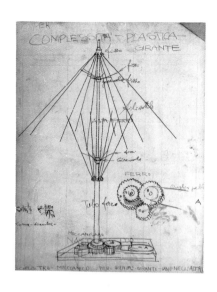

chords that reflect musical chords and tone colors —an allegory of the musician who lives entirely in the realm of tones. A few years later Russolo himself moved into in the field of music with a noise orchestra. This pioneering invention involved the discovery not only of dissonance but of all variety of everyday sounds and noises for musical composition, and made Russolo a forerunner of Concrete Music (see page 69).

Russolo's friend Umberto Boccioni similarly made big-city noise the subject of a painting, *The Street Penetrates into the Building* of 1911 (see page 71). What Russolo would do for the sense of hearing with his "intonarumori", or noise instruments, Boccioni visualized in a typical everyday metropolitan scene. A woman has emerged from a balcony door and stepped up to the railing to be engulfed in the cacophony of the street—the noise and movements of construction workers and their power tools, bright lights, and a plethora of impressions from neighboring buildings. Abandoning the traditional means of realism,

Fortunato Depero (1892–1960)
Rotating Plastic Complex
(*Complessità plastica girante*), 1914
India ink on paper, 30 × 24 cm
Galleria Museo Depero, Rovereto

Fortunato Depero
Project for a Mobile Stage Set
(*Progetto di scena mobile*), 1918
Ink on paper, 29.8 × 39.2 cm
Museo Depero, Rovereto

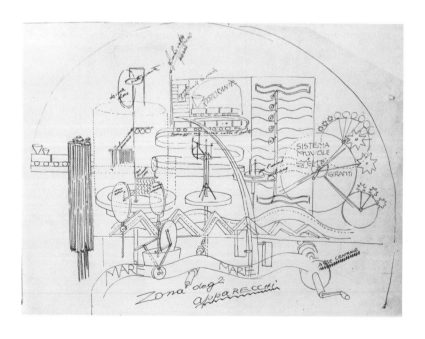

Boccioni employs a restless new visual idiom to capture the simultaneity of visual and auditory perceptions and translate them into a complex network of interpenetrating fragments of motifs and colored shapes. He also uses the bird's-eye, comprehensive view, a Futurist device that breaks through the invisible wall erected by classical linear perspective between picture and viewer. The spectacle of the urban environment and its polyphonic impressions seems to leap out towards us, prompting us to involuntarily identify with the figure of the woman leaning over the railing.

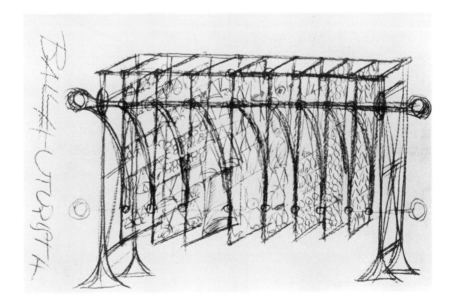

Fortunato Depero
*Colored Plastic Simultaneous Motorized Noise
Complex of Decomposition into Layers
(Complesso plastico colorato motorumorista
simultaneo di scomposizione a strati)*, 1915
Photograph of a lost sculpture, after a reproduction in the manifesto 'Futurist Re-Creation of the Universe,' March 11, 1915

Giacomo Balla
*Project for a Noise-Musical Instrument
(Progetto per strumento musicale rumorista)*, 1914
Pencil on paper, 31 × 42 cm
Private collection, Rome

"We Futurists, Balla and Depero, want to achieve total fusion, in order to create a happy universe; that is, to create it anew from the ground up.

We shall give the invisible, intangible, weightless, non-perceptible skeleton and flesh. We shall find abstract equivalents for every form and element in the universe, then combine these at the whim of our inspiration into plastic complexes, which we set in motion.... Plastic complexes that simultaneously disintegrate, speak, make noise, ring out ..."

(Balla and Depero, *Futurist Re-creation of the Universe*, March 11, 1915)

As Roland Penrose reports Miró as saying, the inspiration for this painting came from an evening walk with Michel Leiris and Georges Bataille along the Seine, returning from a concert.

Penrose goes on to describe the painting as an eloquent visual document of auditory and visual sensations in which trees (and probably streetlights) take the form of musical spiral waves, an early attempt to translate music into pictorial signs which, in later years, would strongly determine Miró's visual language.

(Roland Penrose, *Joan Miró*, exhibition catalogue, 1964)

Joan Miró (1893–1983)
Music – Seine, Michel, Bataille and Me
(*Musique – Seine, Michel, Bataille et moi*), 1927
Oil on canvas, 81 × 100 cm
Kunstmuseum Winterthur, Volkart-Stiftung

Opposite page:
Joan Miró
Dancer II (*Danseuse II*), 1925
Oil on canvas, 115.5 × 88.5 cm
Galerie Rosengart, Lucerne

In conformity with Marinetti's programmatic manifestos, the initially still strong emphasis on motifs in Futurist art increasingly made way for a disintegration of forms and their transmutation into energy-charged lines like those in a magnetic field. Rhythms and dynamic motions were, so to speak, filtered out of the objective context and translated into a diagram of vectors. Already by 1914 this change had gone so far that mimetic representation of impressions and processes had been largely supplanted by an abstract topography of signs and lines, or words and slogans, that retained only an attenuated referential function.

Musical and above all acoustic phenomena played an essential role in this regard. Both Russolo and other Futurists occupied themselves with "bruitistic" experiments such as the 1914–15 "motorumoristic," or the sound and motion sculptures of Balla and Depero, which were extolled as a "futuristic re-creation of the universe." Depero's *Plastic Complexes* were tongue-in-cheek machines with parodistic elements that moved, made noise, spouted water or colored smoke—precursors of Jean Tinguely's "metaharmonic" sculptures.

Balla, too, devoted himself intensively to sound-makers during this period, designing in 1914 a "rumoristic" musical instrument (see page 73). Especially revealing in this connection is his painting *Rumoristica Baltrr*, an innovative synthesis between choreography and musical score. The image represents a diagrammatic record of an actual process. Various physical actions such as walking, ascending stairs, and climbing are indicated by means of simple pointers, accompanied by phonetic syllables suggesting the related sounds (echoing footsteps, a key turning in a lock, the squeak of a window being opened). Though painted on canvas, the image might be a design for a kinetic and acoustic sculpture, or conceivably

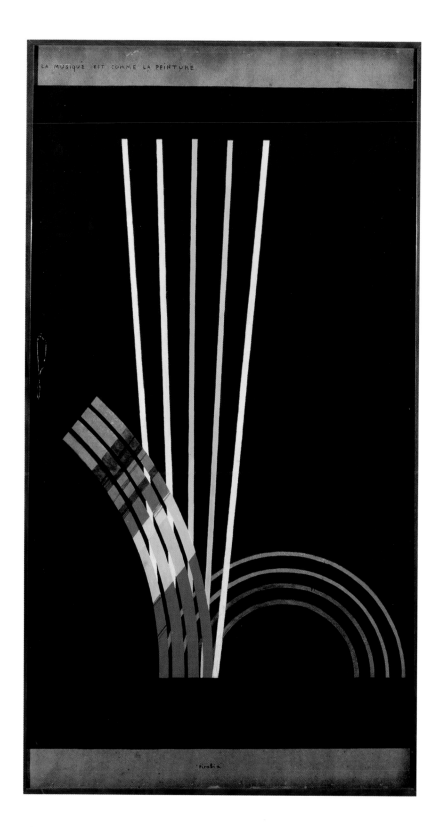

Inspired by a schematic drawing in a physics textbook demonstrating the effect of a magnetic field on alpha, beta and gamma particles *Music is Like Painting* is an encoded image that programmatically illustrates Picabia's conception of painting as a creation of the mind and spirit, independent of objective visible reality, and thus akin to music.

[handwritten margin notes: Stage / Ballet / ↓ / sounds of feet / + music / – foxtrot etc ..]

even for a performance. It anticipates the 1917 performance in Rome of Stravinsky's *Fireworks*, for which Balla created a first, completely abstract mise en scène in which polychrome sculptures and lighting effects took over the actors' roles.

Thus in the twilight zone between art and music the Futurists provided a number of impulses that would prove crucial for subsequent developments. These included, on the one hand, the invention and construction of noise instruments, kinetic-acoustic sculptures, and abstract stage designs *[handwritten: Stage]* (in which field, apart from Balla, Depero and Prampolini were especially active); on the other, Futurism introduced an innovative choreography of pictorial elements which would later be taken up by the Dadaists and Surrealists and anticipated things to come. Instances are Picabia's drawing *Danseuse Jasmine* of 1920, and Miró's painting *Danseuse II* of 1925 (see page 75), both of which record the movements and pirouettes of dancers in the form of choreographic diagrams, which in turn recall the *Floor Geometries* conceived by Schlemmer for his *Triadic Ballet*. The line extends all the way to Warhol, whose *Dance Step* paintings of 1962 almost made art danceable. Transferring to canvas the step sequences of foxtrot or tango in the form of schematic diagrams like those used in dance studios or instruction manuals, Warhol suggested that viewers might try out the steps themselves, on a sheet of glass placed over the canvas on the floor.[47]

Francis Picabia (1879–1953)
Music is Like Painting
(*La Musique est comme la peinture*), 1914–17
Watercolor and gouache on wood, 122 × 66 cm
Collection Manoukian, Paris

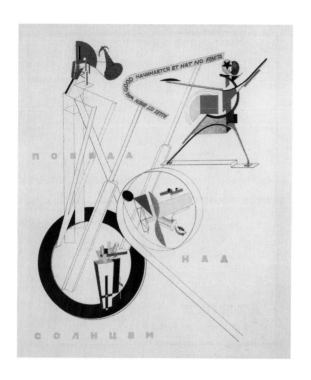

"The present piece is the fragment of a work done in Moscow in 1920–21.... On a square that is open and accessible from all sides we shall build a scaffold, the machinery for the show. This scaffold gives the pieces in the play the opportunity for every possible movement ... They glide, roll, hover within and above the scaffold. All parts of the scaffold and every piece in the play can be set in motion by means of electromechanical forces and equipment, and the controls will be in the hands of a single person. This is the play's director. His place is at the midpoint of the scaffold, at the center of all the energies. He directs movements, sound, and light. He switches on the radio megaphone, and over the square sounds the cacophony of railroad stations, the roaring of Niagara Falls, the hammering of a rolling mill. Light beams follow the movements of the pieces, refracted through prisms and reflections.... The sun as a symbol of ancient universal energy will be torn down from the sky by modern man, who by dint of his technical mastery creates an independent source of energy. This idea of the opera is interwoven with a simultaneity of happenings. The language is alogical. Certain vocal parts are sound-poems."

(El Lissitzky, from the preface to the portfolio)

Synesthetic Investigations of the Russian Vanguard

Russian artists had long felt a special affinity with music. Kandinsky's visual thinking and activity remained closely linked with music throughout his career, as seen in the large-format composition *Fugue* of 1914 (see page 31), or the painting *Counter-Sounds* of 1924, to give only two examples. Similarly, the icon-like, semi-abstract faces depicted by his compatriot, Alexei von Javlensky, bear titles such as *Fugue in Blue and Red* (see page 35) or *Symphony in Black and Red*. Marc Chagall's visual universe gives the impression of a sound-filled cosmos populated at every hand by street musicians and hovering violin players. The examples extend from 1911 and the series of monumental violinists that culminated in *The Green Fiddler*, to 1970 and one of Chagall's last paintings, *Memory of The*

El Lissitzky (1890–1941)
Victory over the Sun (Sieg über die Sonne)
(Electromechanical Show in Sculptural Form)
Opera libretto by A. Krutchonych, 1913,
Hanover, 1923
Figurine portfolio with ten color lithographs
and graphically designed title page,
53.5 × 45.5 cm
Kunsthalle Bielefeld

Opposite page:
Ivan Puni (1892–1956)
The Musician (Le Musicien), 1921
Oil on canvas (two parts sewn together
vertically), 145 × 98 cm
Private collection, Zurich

Iwan Puni

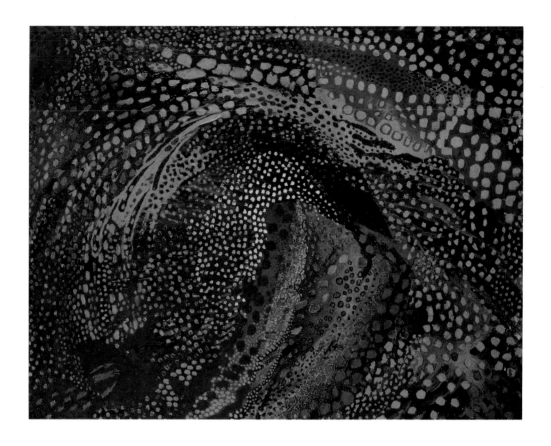

Michail Matyushin (1861–1934)
Painterly-Musical Construction, 1918
Gouache on cardboard, 51.5 × 63.7 cm
Collection of George Costakis, Athens
(Courtesy Angelica Rudenstine,
Princeton, Conn.)

Magic Flute. Ivan Puni put a musician who seems to have become one with his stringed instrument in the center of his 1921, collage-like composition *The Musician*. Kasimir Malevich designed sets and costumes for the Futurist opera *Victory over the Sun*, composed by Michail Matyuchin after a poem by Alexander Krutchonyck. These consisted of "large, flat configurations—triangles, circles, machine parts. The actors wore masks that resembled to-day's gas masks. The 'likari' [performers] looked like running machines. The costumes were constructed cubistically, of cardboard and wire. This altered human anatomy—the performers' movements were limited and determined by the rhythm [established by] the designer and director. The *Song of the Anxious People* (in soft tones) and that of the Pilot (which consisted only of consonants) made a special impression on the audience;

"We declare ... that the following principles are shared in common by painting, poetry and music:
1) Spontaneous spectrum
2) Spontaneous depth
3) Autonomy of tempi as a method of embodying rhythms which are undisputable...."

(From a poster-manifesto of the Russian Futurists, January 1914, St. Petersburg)

"It is rhythm that essentially determines structure, and all spatial relations are subordinate to it."

(Rodchenko, *The Structure of Pictorial Space*, 1920)

Alexander Michailovitch Rodchenko
(1891–1956)
Expressive Rhythm, 1943–44
Gouache on paper, 61 × 172.7 cm
Collection of George Costakis, Athens
(Courtesy Angelica Rudenstine, Princeton, Conn.)

they were sung by experienced performers.... The basic theme of the play is a defense of technology, especially aviation. The victory of technology over the cosmic forces and over biologism. We shall lock the sun/into a concrete building!"[48]

Ten years thereafter El Lissitzky returned to this opera project, creating Suprematist, abstract designs for a ramified performance he described as a "plastic design for an electro-mechanical show." (See page 78). The work was published in 1923 in Hanover, as a portfolio of ten colored lithographs, but was never staged. The painter–musician Matyuchin, who composed the music for the opera and later wrote quarter-tone compositions for violin and piano, taught in the 1920s at the Free State Art Studios and in 1923 became head of the Institute for Ortanic Culture at the GINCHUK in Petrograd. At this period he staged a series of experimental multimedia works such as *The Birth of Light and Volumes* in 1923, and in collaboration with his students systematically investigated the interaction of color and sound. Works created at the time by Matyuchin and the siblings Boris, Mariya, Xenia, and Juri Ender were exhibited in 1926–27 in Petrograd and Warsaw, where they aroused great interest. These works reflected an intensive involvement with the reciprocal relationships among form, color, and sound.

form, color,
sound, light,
space ...

Matyuchin's investigations in this intermediate zone, which he conceived of as a sort of relativity theory of forms, colors, sounds, light, space, and motion, and systematized in tabular form, were based—similar to his quarter-tone compositions— on the principle of division. He penetrated to the tiniest still distinguishable gradations of tones and colors in an attempt to find a common denominator between them. "The wave oscillations of sound are the same as those of color," Matyuchin concluded in 1926. "A thin, dense, transparent, bright, or matte sound clearly shows that our eye as it were hears, and our ear as it were sees."[49]

In Moscow, it was Alexander Rodchenko who studied analogies to the movements of music, in the context of an analysis of the principles of pictorial construction conducted at the WcHUTEMAS workshops. This would subsequently, in the early 1940s, result in an astonishing gouache with the title *Expressive Rhythm* (see page 81) which anticipated Pollock. "It is rhythm that essentially determines structure, and all spatial relationships are subject to it," wrote Rodchenko in a 1920 essay on "The Construction of Pictorial Space."[50] He thereby attributed a fundamental meaning to the principle of rhythm, which since Symbolism had played a significant role in poetry, and in painting had determined the treatment of line above all. Rodchenko's colleague at WcHUTEMAS, Alexander Baranoff-Rossiné, had even before World War I emphasized the interaction of visual design and music in a series of paintings and plastic assemblages collectively titled *Symphonies*. With his Optophonic Piano, on the development of which he worked from 1914 onwards, Baranoff-Rossiné became a pioneer of multimedia art.

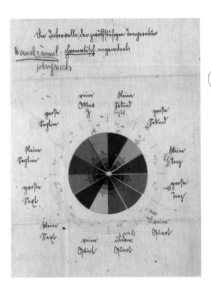

Josef Matthias Hauer (1883–1959)
Conformity of the Twelve-part Color Wheel
with the Intervals of the Twelve-step Scale
(*Übereinstimmung des zwölfteiligen Farbenkreises*
mit den Intervallen der zwölfstufigen Temperatur),
1919–20
For Johannes Itten, with entries by Itten,
27.1 × 20.8 cm
Anneliese Itten, Zurich

Opposite page, top:
Vladimir Baranoff-Rossiné (1888–1944)
The Optophonic Piano
(*Le Piano optophonique*), 1914–20
(Illus.) *Reconstruction of a Painted Disc*
in Original Size,
driven by a small motor, in wooden
framework, 50 × 50 × 16 cm
Collection of Eugène Baranoff-Rossiné, Paris

Opposite page, bottom:
Johannes Itten
Composition of Two Formal Themes,
Dedicated to the Composer Josef Hauer
(*Komposition aus zwei Formenthemen.*
Josef Hauer, dem Komponisten gewidmet), 1917
Oil on canvas, 130 × 70 cm
Stavros Niarchos Collection

Music in Colored Light
and *Harmonia Mundi*

The deeper artists went into the analogy between
colors and musical notes, the more conscious they
became of the limits posed by the paint medium
and the bounded format. Not even the elongated
scroll format could accept much more than a few
bars of music, and the Futurists' diagrams of motion
and noise pressed against the canvas edges as if
striving to break out into the surrounding space.
A transition to three dimensions, to performances,
kinetic and audiovisual experiments suggested itself, especially since attempts to convey color–sound
correspondences by means of colored light projections or cinematographic techniques had a long
tradition. These attempts were closely related to
scientific theories of corresponding sounds and
colors, sound waves and light waves, of the type
already advanced in the seventeenth century by the
universal scholar Athanasius Kircher or the physicist
Isaac Newton. Behind the theories, in turn, stood
the age-old vision of a *harmonia mundi* and a universal music of the spheres, the existence of which
had been derived from proportional correspondences
and formulated in terms of harmonic systems
since Pythagoras, by way of Johannes Kepler.

In the twentieth century such investigations were
continued by Hans Kayser, the Swiss scholar and
author in 1925 of *Orpheus, or Concerning the Sound*
of the World. Morphological Fragments of a General
Harmonics, and *The Hearing Human* in 1930.
Kayser and the composer Josef Matthias Hauer
ardently searched for a formula to describe both
sounds and colors. As Hauer postulated in a 1920
publication, *On the Essence of the Musical*, and
illustrated by trope diagrams developed from
twelve-tone music, both sounds and colors could
"be related to a higher formula, and be derived

from a higher formula, if each only independently
of the other." Painters such as Johannes Itten saw
their synesthetic strivings and attempts to verbalize
them, for example "the quintessence of color is
a dreamlike chiming, is music become light,"[51]
confirmed by the work of Hauer and Kayser.

Colored glass, whose "vertiginous polychrome
musicality" had already inspired Kupka, also struck

Theo van Doesburg (1883–1931)
Composition IV, 1917
Three-part glass window from the residence
of the notary De Lange, Alkmaar,
286 × 56.6 cm
Dienst Verspreide Rijkscollecties, The Hague

other artists as a medium specially suited to design in musical color. Hölzel's stained-glass window sequence of 1915–16 for the Bahlsen Company in Hanover was intended as a "symphony in three movements,"[52] and van Doesburg's three-part glass window for the De Lange house in Alkmaar, completed a year later, was a *Vertical Music* of elementary form–color contrasts based on a Bach fugue.[53]

In France, those who built on the achievements of Delaunay and Kupka included a group around Henri Valensi and Charles Blanc-Gatti, who called themselves "Musicalists" and devoted themselves to interpreting musical compositions in paint. They also developed a harmonic scheme of color–sound correspondences and built audiovisual devices. Paintings such as Valensi's *Spring Symphony* (see page 87) or Blanc-Gatti's *Organ* (see page 89) reflect the cosmological aspect which predominated in the work of many artists during the first decades of the century. By this point music had begun to function on an abstract level—as it had during the Romantic Era—as a metaphor for the invisible and metaphysical, a simile for the sounding cosmos and a universal world harmony.

The Swiss artist Blanc-Gatti, who possessed the innate gift of synopsia, or the hearing of colors, began in the late 1920s to occupy himself with "musical transpositions," visual translations of music pieces from Bach to Stravinsky.[54] His friend, the composer Olivier Messiaen, who owned Blanc-Gatti's canvas *Brilliance* [*Rutilance*], himself made tireless attempts to devise a system of sound chromatics and their interrelationships with color. Messiaen juxtaposed chords that suggested a shift from warm to cold complexes of hues, and developed chord–color tables which were published in his 'Traité du Rhythme, de Couleur, et d'Ornithologie.' In his eyes, all harmonic

Adolf Hölzel (1853–1960)
Left-hand section of the three-part window in the conference room at the headquarters of H. Bahlsen Baking Company, Hanover
Designed: 1915–16; completed: 1918
Each panel: 82 × 60 cm;
overall dimensions: ca. 550 × 200 cm

phenomena could be educed to the phenomenon of resonance, for Messiaen did not believe in man-made tone systems. He associated the effect of being blinded by bright light—a natural occurrence—with the effect of medieval stained glass windows, and raised it to a metaphor for perfect art and a revelation of the divine spirit. "The music of colors," explained Messiaen, "causes what the glass windows and rosettes of the Middle Ages cause: it leads us into blindness. It speaks to our noblest senses, hearing and vision, and at the same time moves our sensibility, stimulates our imagination, heightens our intelligence, and encourages us to overcome our conceptual world and approach that which lies above logic and intuition, namely faith."[55]

The immaterial quality of light, its wave character and relation to sound waves, and its mutability, had centuries before already suggested the idea of creating instruments that simultaneously produced musical notes and colors (in the form of colored light). The Mannerist artist Giuseppe Arcimboldo (1527–93) reputedly invented a musical notation in colors and a sort of zither on which to play it. Around 1725, the Jesuit priest and mathematician Louis-Bertrand Castel built an early color keyboard instrument, about which the composer Georg Philipp Telemann reported in a 1739 essay, "Description of an Eye-Organ or the Eye-Harpsichord Invented by the Famous Herr Pater Castel." While this much-touted invention apparently never got beyond the experimental stage, an anonymous friend and adept of Castel actually built, in 1757 in London, an Eye-Harpsichord with "five hundred lamps behind a row of fifty glass ports" which opened when the keys were struck. As a note on the harpsichord was heard, a "flash of color" was simultaneously emitted through the colored glass of the ports. In 1870 the physicist Frédéric Kastner constructed his Pyrophone, an organ with glass

Henri Valensi (1883–1960)
Symphonie vitale
Dimensions and whereabouts unknown
Exhibited in the 'Salon des Réalités Nouvelles,'
Paris, 1953

After this composition Valensi developed, based on his method of Ciné-Peinture, a film of the same name which was first shown in 1960, at the Compagnie des Lampes, Paris.

Henri Valensi
Spring Symphony (Symphonie printanière), 1932
Oil on canvas, 95 × 130 cm
Collection of Edouard Warin, Paris

cylinders filled with gas which produced tones. This invention was succeeded by the light organs of Bainbridge Bishop, an American in 1888 and Wallace Rimington, an Englishman in 1895.[56]

Prometheus—A Poem of Fire by the Russian composer Alexander Skriabin envisaged the use of a color keyboard to transpose the "luce voice" of the composition into colored light projections. Skriabin associated the twelve tones of the chromatic scale with twelve colors, which changed in conjunction with the basic tones of the harmonies. The premiere performance in Moscow in 1911 did not yet include a color piano, but the first New York performance in 1915 was apparently accompanied by projections produced by a light manual consisting of colored bulbs.

Skriabin's *Prometheus*, on which the Blue Rider Almanach reported, not only inspired Kandinsky's

Charles Blanc-Gatti (1890–1966)
Brilliance (Rutilance), 1940s
Oil on canvas
Collection of Yvonne Loriod-Messiaen, Paris

stage project *The Yellow Sound* but also sparked
off a wave of inventions of audiovisual instruments, including Thomas Wilfred's Clavilux.
In 1923 the Russian painter Baranoff-Rossiné
demonstrated his Optophonic Piano in Moscow,
and the Hungarian Alexander László thrilled
Germany with performances on his Sonochroma-
toscope. At the Bauhaus, Hirschfeld-Mack and
Schwerdtfeger developed Reflector Light Plays,
and in Berlin, Raoul Hausmann worked on his
Optophone. In the United States, the Synchromists
Morgan Russell and Stanton Macdonald-Wright
envisaged a synchromous instrument based
on their color–sound analogies, a machine that
would combine moving colored light with music.[57]
Yet decades of experiments would have to pass
before Macdonald-Wright actually built, in 1960,
a Synchromous Kineidoscope, which was capable of translating the forms and colors of any

Charles Blanc-Gatti
Organ (Orgue), 1930
Oil on canvas
Collection of Yvonne Loriod-Messiaen, Paris

modern painting into a formal arrangement of movements and pure, saturated colors of the light spectrum.[58] The underlying rhythm and dynamics were musically activated by induced kinesis. The Swiss artist Charles Blanc-Gatti also patented, in

1933, a Chromophonic Orchestra designed to "represent mobile, multicolored lighting effects on a screen... in absolute synchrony with a musical piece."[59]

Skriabin's *Prometheus*, an utopian vision in the Wagnerian spirit, was surpassed by his *Temple of the Mysteries*. This composition in turn found a continuation of the project for a temple of colored light in continually changing projections on the interior of the cupola, worked out by the Russian twelve-tone composer Ivan Vyshnegradsky during World War II.

Wendelin Weissheimer (1836–1910)
Photograph of Weissheimer at the Pyrophone
Richard-Wagner-Museum, Bayreuth

László's color projectors (historical photograph)

Model of color piano for the part of Luce
in Scriabin's *Prométhée*, built by A. Mosew

With the emergence in the late 1950s of Kinetic Art, under the banner of "Light and Motion," numerous, increasingly technically sophisticated instruments were developed, such as the Musiscope of Nicolas Schöffer or the Optophonium of Hermann Goepfert. By the late twentieth century, the sound-and-light display has become a mundane discotheque reality, and artists working in the field have tended to shift their focus to large-scale urban projects, many of the recent ones conceived with the aid of digital or laser technology.[60]

Alexander László (b. 1895)
Color-musical performance
(after a watercolor by Matthias Holl),
from *Color-Light Music* (*Die Farblichtmusik*)
by A. László, Leipzig, 1925

"Color-light music seeks to merge two previously separate art genres,
art in notes—i.e. music—with art in colors—i.e. painting—into a
higher unity, a new art.... László determines ... the basic color of a
musical piece, calls one of them 'Preludes for Colored Light and
Piano Blue,' another 'Red,' and retains this basic color throughout
the entire piece. Depending on the changing musical events, such
as dynamic or rhythmical changes, or the appearance of new themes
or a new key, the basic color is supplemented by new color hues,
new 'color keys,' which vary the former in a way that can be best
understood by analogy to the rules of musical variation. The colors
are in turn occasionally supplemented by parallel phenomena to
certain musical figures, plastic configurations such as wavy lines or
wedge shapes. It should be emphasized that this new 'comprehensive
work of art' can not be judged solely either from a musical or a
painterly point of view.... The colors are projected on a backdrop
on a darkened stage by means of a 'color-light piano' consisting of
seven different projectors, developed by László himself and manu-
factured by the Ernemann Company, Dresden; they are controlled
from a console by means of a keyboard...."

(*Introduction to the Color-Light Music of Alexander László*, Leipzig, 1926)

One of a total of 59 studies for the film project of 1913, *Rhythme Coloré*, now in the Museum of Modern Art, New York. Twelve further studies are in the Cinémathéque Française, and several others in the possession of the artist's family. Inspired by new directions in abstract and Cubist painting, Survage began to compose dynamic Color-Rhythm Symphonies. He showed them to Apollinaire, who published them in the first issue of his 'Soirées de Paris' (July–August 1914) and celebrated them as the "ninth muse." At the same period Survage submitted a brief description of his project to the Academy of Sciences in Paris. Despite contacts with the Gaumont Society, which had developed an early color process in 1911, the project was not realized.

Leopold Survage (1879–1968)
Two Studies for *Colored Rhythm*, 1913
Watercolor, brush and ink, 33 × 31 cm each
The Museum of Modern Art, New York

Günter Maas (b. 1923)
Composition XX (Komposition XX), 1966
Private collection

In parallel with developments in the area of light-and-music instruments, artists early on began to interest themselves in cinematographic media as a way of visualizing musical phenomena. Among the pioneers in this field were Leopold Survage, with his *Rhythme Coloré* of 1913, and Duncan Grant, with his abstract-kinetic collage of 1914, which, however, could not yet be translated into cinematic form at that period. Not until the early 1920s did the first films based on painted originals appear, by Eggeling and Richter, whose example inspired others such as Fischinger and Ruttmann. In France, interest in the film medium led to a close collaboration between painters such as Léger, Picabia, Duchamp, and Man Ray, and musicians such as Satie, Milhaud, Antheil, and Varese.

In the 1960s, finally, the Cologne artist Günter Maas made experimental audiovisual films that linked his abstract Sound Paintings with electronic music. Maas employed a device in which photocells traced the painted motifs and transposed them into electronic sounds, producing a transitionless interpenetration of acoustic and visual effects and laying the groundwork for a new synesthetic unity of experience.[61]

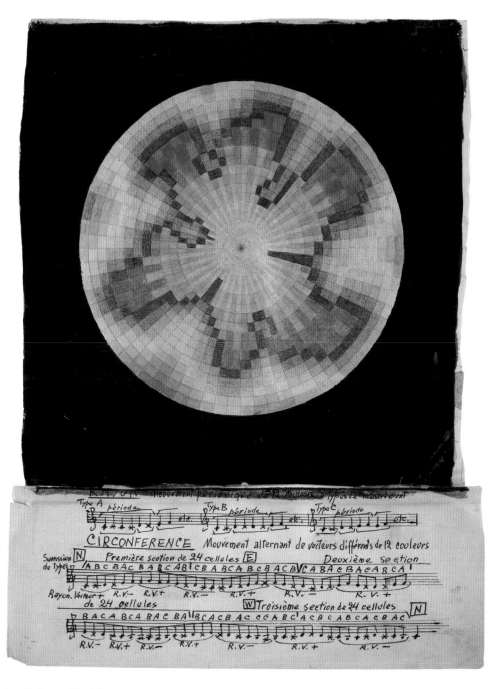

Ivan Vyshnegradsky (1893–1979)
Project for a Temple of Light: Design of Color Arrangement for Cupola Light Projection with Relevant Passage of Score, c. 1943–44
Colored pencil, watercolor and pen and ink on paper, 32 × 24.5 cm each
Private collection

Dance Analogies and "Absolute Rhythm"

Camille Claudel (1864–1943)
The Waltz (La Valse), 1891–1905
Bronze, height 25 cm
Bayerische Staatsgemäldesammlung
Neue Pinakothek, Munich

Gino Severini (1883–1965)
*Dynamics of Form: Light in Space
(Dinamismo di forme: luce nello spazio)*, 1913–14
Oil on canvas, 100 × 73 cm
Galleria Nazionale d'Arte Moderna
e Contemporanea, Rome

Even before the turn of the century, dance, which unites music and rhythmical movement, had become a favorite subject of art, and was treated in a range of approaches extending from Seurat's painting *Chahut* to Camille Claudel's sculpture *La Valse*. For the artists of Classical Modernism as well, the dance provided a stimulus to innovation. A case in point is Severini's vague recollection of a female dancer, which inspired a whole series of pictures that took him to the verge of abstraction. In early 1913, during a seaside holiday, the sight of sunlight glittering on the waves reminded Severini of a dancer in a sequined dress. This spontaneous association provided the basis for his theory of analogies, which he set down that same autumn in a manifesto, *The Pictorial Analogies of Dynamism.* In the wake of this epiphany he attempted in his paintings to create synoptical mergers of ever more diverse ideas and memory images, in innovative equations such as Sea + Dancer = Bouquet of Flowers. By about 1913–14 the rhythmical structures and evocations of colored light had become so far divorced from the seminal motif that the pure idea of dancing motion and glittering, sequined wavelets took on a life of its own, metamorphosed into a weightless staccato of forms and luminous colors whose dynamism even encroached upon the picture frame. With this imagery Severini achieved a new complexity of visual superimpositions and levels of meaning, a painterly polyphony that corresponded to the prediction Marinetti had made for literature in 1912: "Only through extremely extended analogies can an orchestral style that is simultaneously polychrome, polyphonic, and polymorphous comprehend the life of matter...."[62]

Harsher, both more fragmented and more sculptural, were the compositions of the English

Jasper Johns (b. 1930)
Dancer on a Plane, 1980–81
Oil and acrylic on canvas, with polychrome,
relief bronze frame, 200 × 162 cm
(including frame)
The Tate Gallery, London

The painting is an homage to Merce
Cunningham (b. 1919), dancer and choreog-
rapher and one of the artist's closest friends, for
whose troupe Johns has designed numerous
sets and costumes since the 1950s.

Vorticists, who, like David Bomberg and Wyndham
Lewis, concerned themselves very intensively with
the dance and with its translation into abstract
terms. Their spokesman, Ezra Pound, proclaimed
with respect to his free-verse poetry that he believed
in "absolute rhythm," and that he and his artist–
friends used form like musicians used sound.
They did not imitate the wood dove, he went on,
but combined and articulated tones or forms into
Bachian fugues or colored arrangements, or interrelated planes.[63] Pictures and studies such as Lewis's
Red Duet of 1914, Bomberg's *Under Coercion* of
1913–14, or William Roberts's *Two Step* of around
1915, evinced visual correspondences with Pound's
credo.

Even the artists of De Stijl, whose serene compositions could hardly have been more different
from the Vorticists' or Futurists', were animated
by the idea of an "absolute rhythm." Van Doesburg, co-founder of the group, addressed the
theme as early as 1916 in a painting titled *Heroic
Movement*, couching it in an abstract, symbolic
form that still recalled the romanticism of Art
Nouveau. Yet just two years later his visual idiom
changed completely. Out of systematic motion
studies of a dancer van Doesburg distilled a colored framework of vertical and horizontal elements
whose rhythmical arrangement on the white plane
was intended to evoke the stamping rhythms of
the Cossack dance. The following compositions
were more reserved, for instance *Tarantella* or
Composition in Grey, which was originally titled
Ragtime, and in which the rhythmic scansion was
shifted into light–dark contrasts. Then, as a result
of his search for a formula adequate to his dynamic view of the world as being involved in
"incessant transformation," van Doesburg abandoned the static, gravity-oriented De Stijl principle
of orthogonal structure. He embarked upon compositions with diagonals which—like the monu-

Inspired by the performances of the Russian Ballet in London and the onset of jazz fever in Europe, but especially by Valentine de Saint-Point's fascinating dance performances with light projections and shadow plays, no genre more deeply concerned the English avant-garde and encouraged its striving for a complete unity of form and content than dance. In their studies and paintings of 1913–15 they attempted to visually translate the concept of "absolute rhythm" advanced by their literary spokesman, Ezra Pound, as the credo of Vers libre, or free verse.

"I believe in an absolute rhythm, which would exactly conform to the feeling or shade of feeling it was meant to convey. A person's rhythm must be essential, the poet added, and therefore basically intrinsic and unique—not imitated, inimitable."

(Ezra Pound, *Prolegomena*, 1912)

William Roberts (1895–1980)
Study for Two Step II, c. 1915
Pencil, watercolor and gouache, 30 × 23 cm
Collection of Anthony d'Offay, London

Wyndham Lewis (1882–1957)
Red Duet, 1914
Chalk and gouache on paper, 38.5 × 56 cm
Collection of Anthony d'Offay, London;
formerly collection of Ezra Pound

mental *Contra-Composition VI* in *Dissonances* of 1925—condensed his conception of a continually changing, dynamic space– time continuum into a concise formula. In his decorations in the dance hall at Café Aubette in Strasbourg, van Doesburg's contrasting diagonal rhythms carried over directly into the space.

Though the theme of dance did not explicitly enter Mondrian's œuvre until 1929–30 in the two *Foxtrot* paintings in the Yale Art Gallery, his early *Pier and Ocean* studies already represented something in the nature of stenographic records of wave rhythms on the water surface. His enthusiasm for jazz, expressed in his writings as well as his art, found new nourishment in New York, where Mondrian frequented the famous Downtown jazz clubs. The

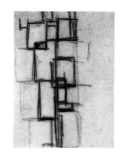

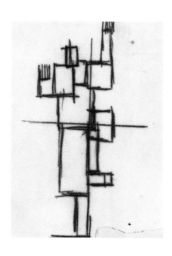
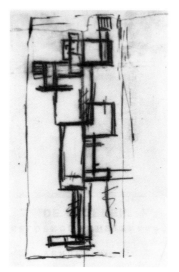
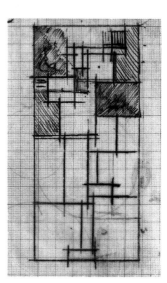

Theo van Doesburg
Seven Studies for the Composition
"Rhythm of a Russian Dance," 1917–18
Pencil, pen and ink,
formats from 8.2 × 6.7 to 20.3 × 13.3 cm
The Museum of Modern Art, New York

years 1941 to 1944 saw the emergence of his legacy
to posterity, the two *Boogie Woogie* paintings, in
which not only the syncopated rhythms of jazz but
the experience of Manhattan and its street grid and
flickering neon signs found congenial expression.
This unity of musical and pictorial rhythms was
immediately felt by Mondrian's contemporaries, as
evinced by the compelling interpretation of James
Johnson Sweeney. "The eye," Sweeney wrote, "was
led with varying velocity from one group of color
gradations to the next. Simultaneously, and in
contrast to the endless mutability of the smaller
motifs, the image was dominated by a constant

Theo van Doesburg
Rhythm of a Russian Dance, 1918
Oil on canvas, 135.9 × 61.6 cm
The Museum of Modern Art,
New York

Piet Mondrian (1872–1944)
Broadway Boogie-Woogie, 1942–43
Oil on canvas, 127 × 127 cm
The Museum of Modern Art, New York

"I view boogie-woogie as homogeneous with
my intention in painting—a destruction of
melody equivalent to the destruction of natural
appearances, and construction by means of a
continual confrontation of pure means—
dynamic rhythms."

(Mondrian, interview with James Johnson
Sweeney, c. 1943)

repetition of the right-angle theme, which droned
like an incessant double-bass rhythm through a
sprinkling of rapid arpeggios and lissom clarinet
notes."[64]

The release of absolute rhythm and its visualization
through an elementary vocabulary reduced to a
few forms and colors anticipated the beginnings of
serial imagery. It also pointed the way for American
Constructivists such as Burgoyne Diller, and for
the European protagonists of Concrete Art.

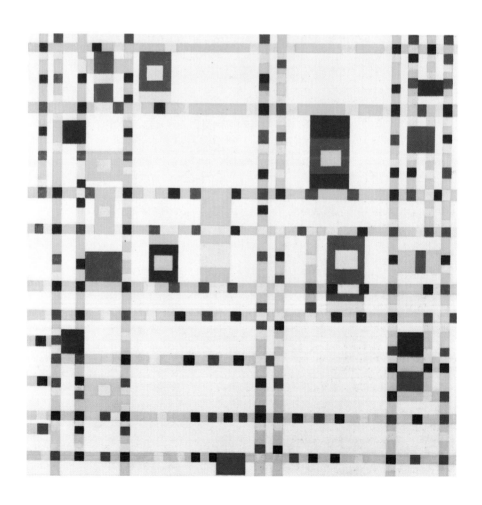

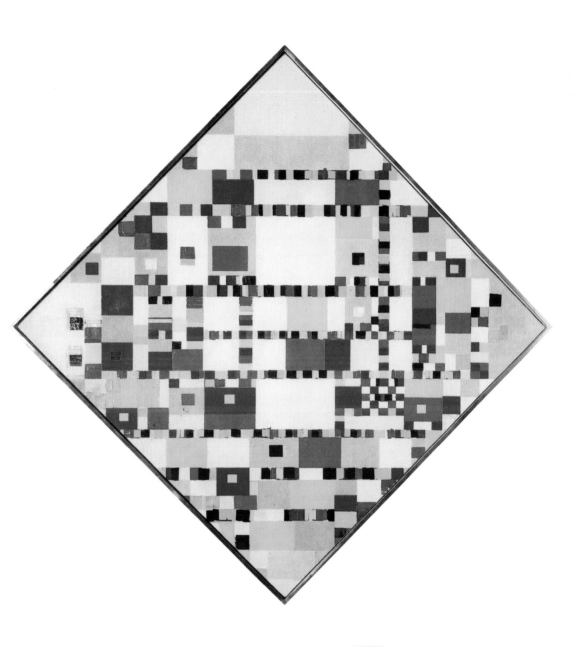

Piet Mondrian
Victory Boogie-Woogie, 1942–43
Oil on canvas with colored tape and paper,
126.1 × 126.1 cm
Gemeentemuseum, The Hague

"A reduction of form and color, a liberation of form and color from
their particular associated phenomena in nature, is necessary to
liberate rhythm and consequently art. Purified rhythm produces
purified equilibrium.... Whether obscured or purified, rhythm produces
dynamic movement through continual confrontation of elements of
the composition.... In every art it is the function of rhythm to prevent
statically bound expression through dynamic action."

(Mondrian, *Liberation from Oppression in Art and Life,* 1941)

Dance Analogies and "Absolute Rhythm"   101

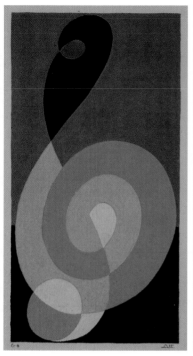

different artists

The Serial Principle
and Transformed Material

Mondrian's rigorously systematic compositions
with their limitation to the three primary colors,
yellow, red, and blue, and the two non-colors black
and white, disposed in a coordinate system of
horizontals and verticals, can be linked to such
principles of Schoenberg's serial technique as
symmetry, inversion, or retrogression.[65] If the early,
atonal Schoenberg found a correspondence in
Kandinsky, serial music found an approximation in
Mondrian. Across the board, in fact, an increasing
tendency towards rationalization made itself felt in
both art and music from the late 1920s onwards.
Just as Schoenberg and Webern codified the harmonic system of the twelve-tone series, Kandinsky,
Klee, and Albers developed fundamental theories

Josef Albers (1888–1976)
Treble Clef, from *Treble Clef G2–G7*, 1935
Six gouaches, 36.5 × 20.5 cm each
Josef Albers Museum, Bottrop

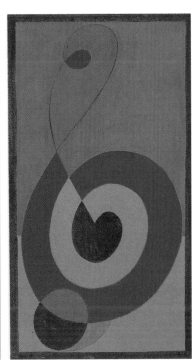

The first group of logically developed, serial works in Albers's oeuvre.

"Only by alterations in color can a completely different climate be engendered.... Every color gives and takes from the others.... What I envisage is playing 'staccato' or 'legato'—and all the other musical terms."

(Albers, interview with Katherine Kuh, 1960)

"As long as we hear only the individual notes in a piece of music, we do not hear music at all. The hearing of music depends on perceiving 'between the notes,' their vertical and horizontal distance."

"We are concerned ... with the interaction of color, i.e, seeing what happens between the colors."

(Albers, Interaction of Color, 1963)

of art at the Bauhaus. These were systematic conclusions derived from an analysis of their earlier improvisations which, in Albers's case, culminated in serial groups of works such as the *Treble Clef* sequence of 1934. The isolation of elements and their deployment in a systematic way corresponded, in the field of music, to the isolation of sounds and their egalitarian treatment in serial composition.

Nor did music always play the giving part in this complex process of parallel developments and cross-pollenations. This is illustrated by the example of Russolo, who in a 1913 manifesto advocated an art of sounds, *L'Arte dei Rumori*, and whose noise instruments and noise concerts already put into practice what was later envisaged by composers such as Antheil, Milhaud, Honegger, and especially Varese (who indeed no longer recognized any distinction between noise and sound).

L'ART DES BRUITS

Manifeste futuriste

Mon cher Balilla Pratella, grand musicien futuriste,

Le 9 Mars 1913, durant notre sanglante victoire remportée sur 4000 passéistes au Théâtre ostanzi de Rome, nous défendions à coups de poing et de canne ta **Musique futuriste**, exécutée par un orchestre puissant, quand tout-à-coup mon esprit intuitif conçut un nouvel art que, seul, ton génie peut créer: l'Art des Bruits, conséquence logique de tes merveilleuses innovations.

La vie antique ne fut que silence. C'est au dix-neuvième siècle seulement, avec l'invention des machines, que naquit le Bruit. Aujourd'hui le bruit domine en souverain sur la sensibilité des hommes. Durant plusieurs siècles la vie se déroula en silence, ou en sourdine. Les bruits les plus retentissants n'étaient ni intenses, ni prolongés, ni variés. En effet, la nature est normalement silencieuse, sauf les tempêtes, les ouragans, les avalanches, les cascades et quelques mouvements telluriques exceptionnels. C'est pourquoi les premiers sons que l'homme tira d'un roseau percé ou d'une corde tendue, l'émerveillèrent profondément.

Les peuples primitifs attribuèrent au son une origine divine. Il fut entouré d'un respect religieux et réservé aux prêtres qui l'utilisèrent pour enrichir leurs rites d'un nouveau mystère. C'est ainsi que se forma la conception du son comme chose à part, différente et indépendante de la vie. La

It was no coincidence that the impulse for "Bruitismo" came from a painter. The principle of collage, the integration in art of objets trouvés, existing materials, and things as practiced by the Cubists, Futurists, and Dadaists, was adapted for music by Stravinsky, Satie, and others in the form of collage quotations, whereby natural or mechanical noises were employed as a new source of auditory material. Similarly, the integration of letters and typographic material in painting can be linked with the autonomy accorded to tones and sounds, speech articulations, and recitative in the new music. After first forays into the frontier region between speech and music by the Russian Futurists, explorations were continued by pioneers like Raoul Hausmann with his sound poems and Kurt Schwitters with

Luigi Russolo
The Art of Noise (*L'Art des bruits*),
Manifesto, March 11, 1913
28.9 × 22.9 cm
Private collection, Stuttgart

Kurt Schwitters (1887–1948)
My Sonata in Primal Sounds
(*Meine Sonate in Urlauten*).
i 10, Internationale Revue, vol. I, no. 11,
Nov. 1927.
First part of Schwitters's "Ursonate"
(here still entitled "Sonata in Urlauten")
with the artist's explanations
Staatsgalerie Stuttgart (Library)

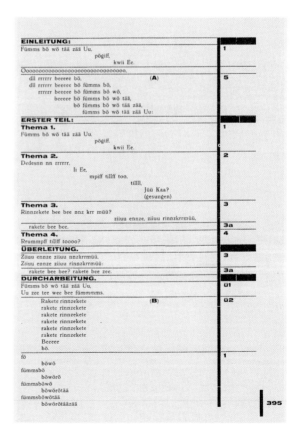

"My sonata in primal sounds is built up on the first movement, a rondo with the main theme of 'fümms'.... This main theme was partially derived from a poem by Raoul Hausmann, which ... was originally, as far as I know, only a trial proof for the selection of type faces.... As Dadaist and arbitrary the compiling of themes and inspirations was, just as rigorous was the intrinsic logic, strictness, and consequence of the development and grouping. The sonata consists of four movements, a prelude, a finale, and, seventh, a cadence in the fourth movement. The first movement is a rondo with four main themes.... The rhythm is strong and weak, loud and soft, compressed and distended, etc., as you yourself will have noticed. Explaining the fine variations and compositions of the themes would, in the long run, be boring, and might well detract from the enjoyment of reading and listening...."

(Schwitters, 1927)

his *Ursonate,* and finally resulted in the genre of "phonetic poetry."

Ever since the invention of collage, which Picasso already expanded into three-dimensional assemblage in his *Violins* of 1912–13, the factor of the materials employed took on a continually increasing importance in the aesthetics of both art and music. With the discovery of the found object and the readymade, new dimensions opened up for both arts. Man Ray, for example, used photomontage to transform a female nude into a violin (see page 106), or fitted an actual double-bass neck with a shock of horsehair to evoke a woman's head with a ponytail. The expansion of the definition of art now permitted almost anything to be used as

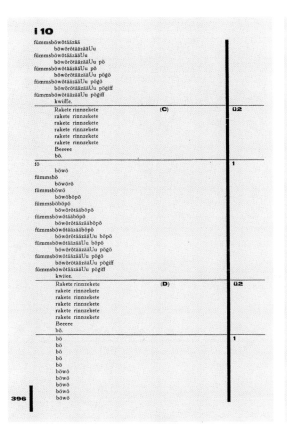

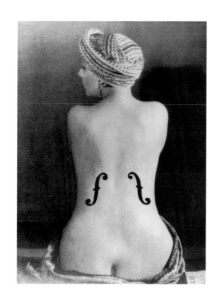

material, limited only by the artist's skills in instrumentalizing it. Just as the painted image gradually took on the character of a musical score, the object could made over into an instrument, the instrument converted into a figure and vice versa, whereby the process of aesthetic metamorphosis became ever more important in its own right.

Exploration of instrumental metamorphoses was initially a domain of the Dadaists and Surrealists, from Marcel Duchamp through Max Ernst to René Magritte. When Salvador Dalí evoked traumatic visions in paintings such as *Partial Illusion: Six Apparitions of Lenin on a Piano* of 1931, or *Fountain-Piano* of 1933, he simultaneously triggered surprising acoustic associations—a babbling spring flowing out of a piano, or the sound one imagines

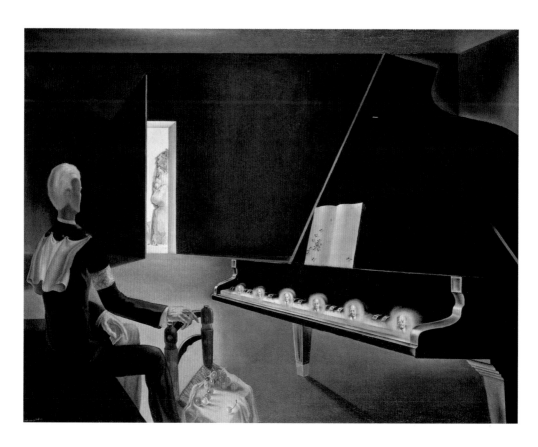

René Magritte (1898–1967)
The Public Fair (*La Fête populaire*), 1961
Watercolor, black chalk and collage,
44 × 36.5 cm
Collection of Leo Castelli, New York

Opposite page, top: Man Ray (1890–1976)
Ingres's Violin (*Violon d'Ingres*), 1924
Original print of altered photograph,
signed by the artist and dedicated to
Hans Richter on the reverse, 15 × 11.1 cm
Collection of Hans Bolliger, Zurich

Bottom: Salvador Dalí (1904–1989)
*Partial Illusion. Six Apparitions of Lenin
on a Grand Piano,* 1931
Oil on canvas, 114 × 146 cm
Musée National d'Art Moderne,
Centre Pompidou, Paris

"The art of painting is an art of thinking.... The purpose of painting
is to activate and intensify vision, based on a purely visual perception
of the outside world.... On the other hand, more than our visual
perception is concerned when nature suddenly reveals threatening
aspects. In this case, the other senses—hearing, touch, smell, taste—
contribute to putting us in a state of panic."

(Magritte, *The True Art of Painting,* 1949)

Joseph Beuys (1921–1986)
Revolution Piano (Revolutionsklavier), 1969
Piano, carnations, roses, 132.5 × 152 × 66 cm
Städtisches Museum Abteiberg,
Mönchengladbach

would be produced by six heads of Lenin bouncing along a keyboard, or playing from sheet music with ants instead of notes (an idea, by the way, that would later reappear in Patterson's *Ant Score*). After World War II, impulses from Dada and Surrealism were taken up especially by the Nouveaux Réalistes and the Fluxus movement. When Arman sawed guitars apart, scorched or smashed pianos, when Günther Uecker studded a piano with nails and painted it, Joseph Beuys sewed a grand piano into a felt cover or inserted flowers between the strings of another, and Nam June Paik prepared a piano such that its sounds were distorted to the

Nam June Paik (b. 1932)
Integral Piano (*Klavier Integral*), 1958–63
Piano, prepared with various
everyday objects, 136 × 140 × 65 cm
Museum Moderner Kunst, Vienna,
Sammlung Wolfgang Hahn

point of unrecognizability, the sound and fury of
these actions were evidently just as significant to
the artists as their results. In such performances
the collage principle lived on, if in the inverted form
of what Wolf Vostell dubbed "dé-collage", and the
destruction of a musical instrument opened up
new paths for both music and visual art.

Marcel Duchamp
Erratum musical, 1913
Ink on music paper, facsimile from
the "Green Box," 1934, 31 × 24 cm
Staatsgalerie Stuttgart, Graphische Sammlung

Score for three voices (Duchamp and his two
sisters, Yvonne and Madeleine), based on a
chance arrangement of notes drawn from a
hat. The text is a dictionary definition of the
verb "imprimer" (to print).

The Intermedia Synthesis

As the two arts became ever more receptive to the
factor of process—painting led by Jackson Pollock,
music led by John Cage—by integrating the production of sound or the making and remaking of the
painted image, they inevitably converged. In 1960
they finally met and mingled in the live collages of
the Fluxus concerts, in which acoustic, visual, and
tactile materials were brought together. Chance and
objet trouvé, silence, speaking, and screaming,
noise, cacophony, and musical sound, passivity
and activity were amalgamated into an audiovisual, multimedia spectacle that, like music, un-
folded in the dimension of time and, except for a
handful of relics, lapsed and vanished again with
time. The barriers between the genres seemed to
have been overcome, art wedded with life.

Many of the people associated with Fluxus were
painters, musicians, and poets in one. Following
in the footsteps of their pathfinder, Duchamp, who
as early as 1913 had based the score of his *Erratum*

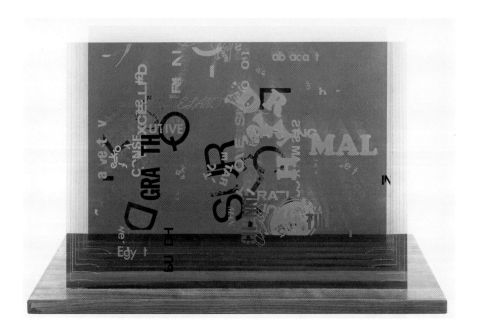

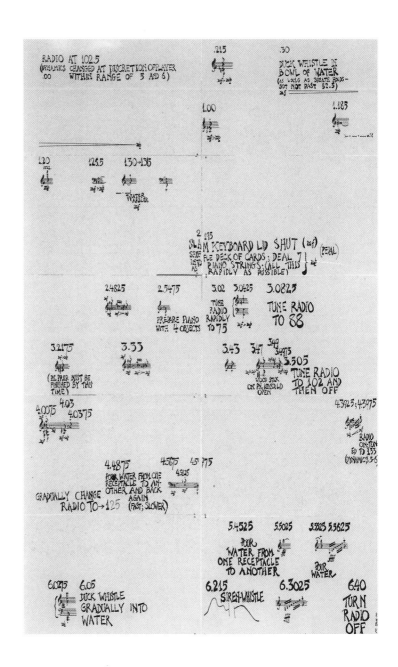

John Cage
Water Music, 1960
Transcription for musicians, publ. by
Edition Peters, New York, 1960

Opposite page:
John Cage (b. 1912)
Not Wanting to Say Anything about Marcel, 1971
Plexigram III of VIII, 8 dark panes of plexiglass,
colored print, in stand, 28.3 × 62.3 × 5.5 cm
Edition Peters, New York

musical on the principle of chance and had devised
a "new musical alphabet" consisting of numbers,
Cage and Allan Kaprow, Beuys and Vostell, Paik and
George Maciunas, Alison Knowles and La Monte
Young, Emmett Williams and Dick Higgins, George
Brecht and Robert Filliou (or Hermann Nitsch)
were borne along by this intermedia wave in the

Yves Klein (1928–1962)
Monotone-Silence Symphony
(*Symphonie monoton-silence*), 1949/61
Blueprint of a handwritten score on
music paper, with handwritten notes
in red and blue ink, 41.7 × 29.5 cm
Private collection

Arrangement of a score, probably with the aid
of the musician Pierre Henri. Scored for twenty
voices and thirty-two instruments.

"His aim was a sound 'divested of both beginning and end. And thus floating in space,
remaining there, re-pervading it, only to issue
in silence.' In 1949 he achieved this in public
for the first time, with a total duration of
20 minutes."

(Paul Wember, *Yves Klein*, 1969)

early 1960s. The pioneers in the field also included
Yves Klein, who had died young. Klein wrote a
One-Note Silence Symphony that consisted of a
sustained D-major chord which seemed to hover
in space until it gave way to a silence that was
sustained for an equal length of time (it was first
performed publicly in 1949). From this melting
pot both arts were to emerge transformed, en-
riched by new, previously undreamed-of aspects
and potentials. Yet the Fluxus innovations attracted
little interest on the so-called serious music scene,
becoming known at best under the marginal rubric
of "experimental music."

It was not long until an escape into previously for-
bidden regions set in. Painting withdrew from
visibility and music ensconced itself in silence.
Out of the Fluxus and Happenings movement,
which had initially revelled in tangible, haptic
materials, grew Conceptual Art, in which the factor
of execution dwindled to near insignificance. The
essential thing now was the idea behind a work,
the concept (here again, shades of Duchamp
appeared). Everything else remained up to the
imagination and creativity of the viewer, who thus
became an interpreter and co-participant in the
work. Dieter Schnebel, Higgins or Gerhard Rühm
made "thinkable music," "music to read," or
"pencil music," audible only in the viewer's mind.

Gerhard Rühm (b. 1930)
Sheet from the Cycle "Duo," 1983
Pencil on music paper, 34 × 54 cm
Private collection

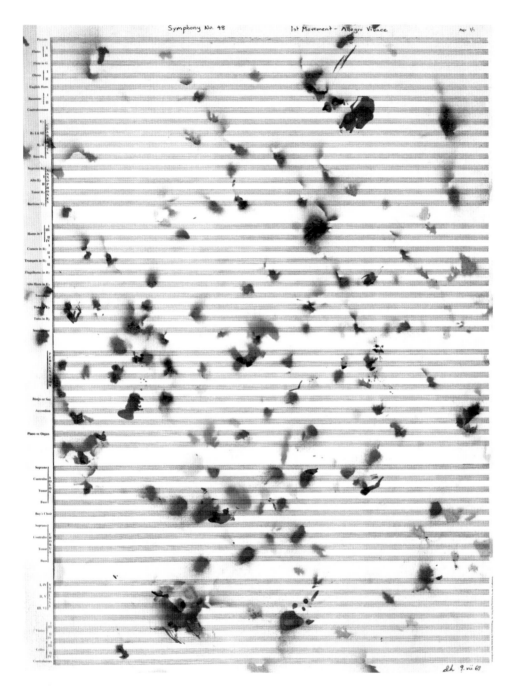

Dick Higgins (b. 1938)
Symphony No. 48, 1969
1st movement—Allegro Vivace
2nd movement—Andante Spicatto
3rd movement—Allegro Grandioso
Paint spatters on music paper,
57 × 44.5 cm each
Gelbe Musik, Berlin

Moritz von Schwind (1804–1871)
Die Katzensymphonie (Le Chat Noir)
(*Cat Symphony [The Black Cat]*), 1868
Pen and brush and dark brown ink over pencil,
pen in light brown ink (music lines) on beige
paper, 31.7 × 21.5 cm
Staatliche Kunsthalle Karlsruhe,
Kupferstichkabinett

Von Schwind presumably dedicated this hu-
moresque "cat score" to the violin virtuoso
Joseph Joachim (1831–1907), on the occasion
of Joachim's nomination as director of the
Berlin College of Music in 1868.

In a letter to F. Senff, a Leipzig music publisher
whom he requested to make reproductions of
the drawing, von Schwind wittily described it as
"this daring attempt to put a more expressive,
spiritualized notation system in the place of
this outmoded, obsolete, pedantic, and dry-
as-dust copycat business."

(Letter of January 4, 1869)

Graphic Music

By way of background to this evolution we should
look briefly at the development of forms of notation,
which played a key role in both arts. Artists took
an early interest in the way composers worked,
with an eye to achieving a comparable autonomy
for their pictorial means and treatment of space
and time. Yet composers apparently did not see
the need to reform their linear notation system
until about 1950, when they realized that its traditional basis in diatonics and metrics was no longer
adequate to the acoustic phenomena of the new
music. (An exception was Moritz von Schwind,
who as early as 1868 found traditional notation so
outmoded that he set out to revolutionize it with
a witty score, *Cat Symphony*.)

The abstract and autonomous visual idiom developed by painters in the previous decades was
now enlisted by musicians to their own ends. And
they very rapidly discovered that musical inspiration
could be channelled in new directions by visual
signs that were no longer bound to the staff but
amounted to space-defining directives. Notation,
which had earlier served merely as an auxiliary
means to record musical ideas with an eye to

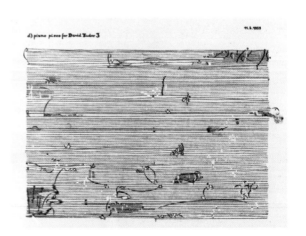

Sylvano Bussotti (b. 1931)
Five Piano Pieces for David Tudor
Universal Edition, London, 1959
Seven sheets, 36 × 27.8 cm
Collection of Erhard Karkoschka, Stuttgart
(Illus.: *Piano piece 3*)

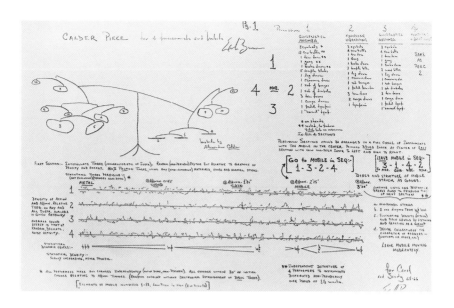

Earle Brown (b. 1926)
Calder Piece, 1965–66
For four percussion groups totalling nearly 100 instruments and a mobile by Calder.
Sheet 1: Pencil on paper, 35.5 × 54 cm
Collection of the artist, New York

Calder Piece was conceived in 1963. But it was only after 1966 and Calder's completion of the mobile *Chef d'Orchestre* at Brown's instigation, that the piece was premiered at the Théâtre de l'Atelier in Paris, in 1967. To Brown's mind, Calder's notion of 'open form' perfectly corresponded to his own compositional concept of 'available forms.' As early as 1961, with reference to his piece *Available Forms II*, he had already explained that the mobility of its elements had been inspired by Calder's mobiles, in which, similarly to this work, basic units were subjected to countless different formal relationships.

In *Calder Piece*, four percussion groups play around and with Calder's Chef d'Orchestre mobile, actually using it as an instrument. The sounds produced, explained Brown, were initially little touches and strikes without resonance. One after the other the percussionists returned to their batteries, playing marimbas, producing harsh, sharp wood tones, accelerating their movements. At their next approach to the mobile it was transformed into vibrating gongs and cymbals.

(Pauli Hayes, "Earle Brown Creates Sound Sculpture," The Aspen Times, July 30, 1981)

their performance, now burgeoned into the visual independence of "musical graphics."

This concept, introduced by a co-founder of this intermediate genre, the composer Roman Haubenstock-Ramati, recalled an article by Oskar Rainer concerning "Musical Graphics: Studies and Experiments on the Reciprocal Relationships between Tone and Color Harmonies," published in 1925 in Vienna. Rainer conducted experiments with laypeople, asking them to create spontaneous drawings to music, and from the results he derived certain criteria for the use of this activity in therapy. He and his successor, Hans Sündermann, were concerned less with the aesthetic quality of these musically inspired images than in the conclusions they could draw from them about the mental state of their authors. The works illustrated in his article evinced astonishing parallels with the abstract paintings of Kandinsky or Kupka, which were unknown to the participants in the experiments.

The crucial impetus for the development of "musical graphics" as an interlinear notation for the new music came from the pressing need for a symbolic

Heinrich Neugeboren
(Henri Nouveau) (1901–1959)
*Sculptural Representation of Bars
52–55 of E-Flat Minor Fugue by
J.S. Bach, Proposal for a Bach
Monument,* 1928
Steel, ca. 60 × 60 cm
Bauhaus-Archiv, Museum für
Gestaltung, Berlin

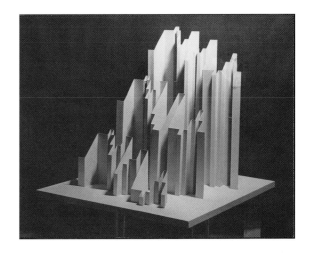

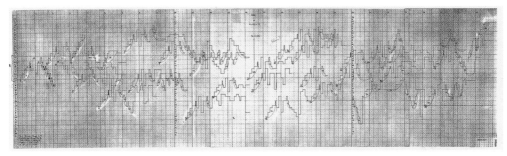

Heinrich Neugeboren
Graphic Depiction of Four-part Fugue No. 1
from "Das wohltemperierte Klavier" by
J.S. Bach, 1928/44
Black india ink (alto and bass)
and red ink (soprano and tenor) on graph
paper, 30 × 112 cm
Bauhaus-Archiv, Museum für Gestaltung,
Berlin

Bars 52–55 of E-Flat Minor Fugue by J.S. Bach

language suited to its new sound effects and sound-producing instruments and equipment. Above all, composers were concerned to expand the scope between notation and performance in order to give those who interpreted their works a greater leeway to lend them openness, flexibility, and complexity of meaning. Earle Brown, whose 1952 compositions *Synergy* and *December* were written for the first time in an interlinear mode, explained the appeal of musical graphics. The mobility or variability of a work should be activated during the performance, as in a Calder mobile, said Brown, and should be spontaneously and intensely expressed by the performers, just as in the immediate contact between

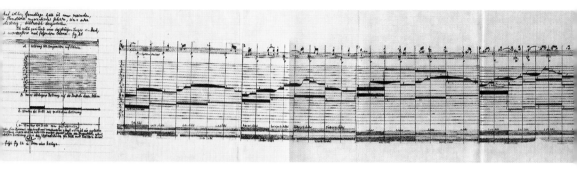

Paul Klee
Transcription of the First Bars of the Adagio,
6th Sonata for Violin and Harpsichord in
G-Major, by Johann Sebastian Bach.
From the "Comments on the Principles of
Formal Design" (Beiträgen zur bildnerischen
Formlehre), Klee's first lecture series at the
Weimar Bauhaus, 1921–22

Homage to the composer Johann Jakob Froberger (b. 1616 in Stuttgart,
d. 1667 in Mömpelgard), whose then extremely innovative approach
to composition and notation, "a very interwoven way of writing,"
became influential all the way down to Bach and Händel.

"His music, despite the lilting joyousness of many a dance mode,
is an extremely inwardly directed art, intimate, elegaic, occasionally
losing itself in sentimentality, and often suffused by a resigned
melancholy."

(Christiane Bernsdorff-Engelbrecht)

Armin Martinmüller (b. 1943)
Hommage à Froberger Opus 225 – Lamentation,
1981–82
Acrylic and tempera on canvas, 75 × 90 cm
Galerie Schlichtenmaier, Grafenau

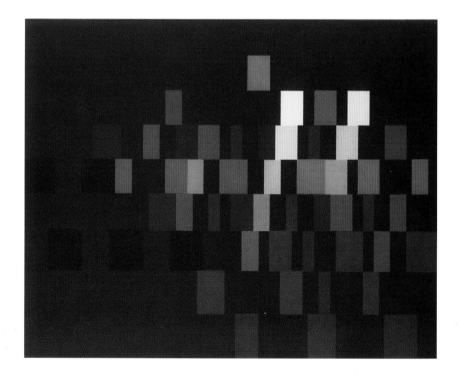

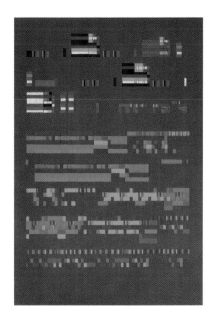

Pollock and his canvases and materials. These two elements, mobility of the sound components within a work and the graphic provocation of an intensive participation on the part of the performers, Brown concluded, were the most fascinating new potentials for "sound objects" analogous to sculpture and painting.[66]

The innovative means of notation since developed include exact instructions and precise sign systems such as those of Karlheinz Stockhausen and András Ligeti, but also imaginative script designs and intuitive visual scores such as those of Sylvano Bussotti, Anestis Logothetis, Haubenstock-Ramati, or Dieter Schnebel, the musical graphic artists *per se*.[67]

Still, composers tend to limit themselves to linear configurations and the black-and-white scale, since they are largely concerned with visualizing structures and links, transitions in tone pitch, articulations, and instrumental differentiations. The temporal process of a musical performance is translated into a spatial configuration, for, as Stockhausen says, "the experience of time can be transposed into an experience of space."[68]

Top:
Robert Strübin (1897–1965)
Music Picture – Stravinsky, a Few Bars from the "Firebird Suite"
(*Musikbild – Strawinsky, Einige Takte aus "Feuervogel"*), c. 1960
Gouache on paper, 80 × 50 cm
Collection of Max Wandeler, Lucerne

Jakob Weder (b. 1906)
Orchestral Suite 3 in D-Major by J.S. Bach, 1980–81
(for two oboes, three trumpets, kettle drum and strings)
Acrylic on canvas,
approx. 122 × 171 cm
Galerie Nicoline Pon, Zurich

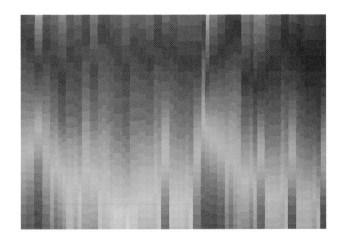

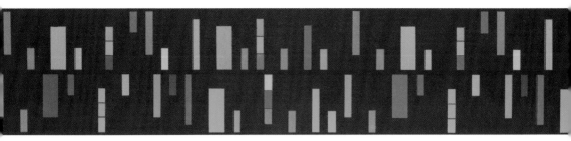

Luigi Veronesi (b. 1908)
Chromatic Visualization: Anton Webern's
"Variations for Piano" Opus 27, Variation II,
Bars 1–19, 1972
Synthetic resin paint on cardboard, 39 × 174 cm
Collection of the artist, Milan

"The composer's original score is the starting point for my formal translations which are deepened by the study of musical theory and musical-historical texts. Only my choice of background images is not made using this system. As such, I can combine Bruckner's paintings and drawings with panoramic views of the Alps and pictures of the Baroque monastery of St. Florian, near Linz in Austria, where Bruckner played the organ, studied, taught, and is buried.

All other formal decisions are directly linked to the systematic translation method. This method is adapted to suit the special requirements of each composition.... All images in the painting are based on color pictures taken by me or other photographers with whom I work.... They were then painted over an arrangement of fiberglass strips on the wall. Depending on the width, each strip represents a particular note of a particular duration. These strips are then rearranged, according to the composition and new painterly information is added while keeping to the score.... Each strip embodies one orchestral chord in the piece.... Later I work in images into the fragmented motifs such as in Bruckner series, in which parts of pictures of St. Florian alternate with parts of views of the Alps. In this way I can illustrate several instruments as well as accentuate the interaction of image and musical motif or idea."

(Jack Ox, *The Systematic Translation of Musical Compositions into Paintings*, 1984)

Jack Ox (b. 1948)
Anton Bruckner – Symphony No. 8
Second painting from the First Movement, 1984
Oil on fiberglass, mounted on nylon vinyl,
119 × 456 cm
Collection of the artist, New York

Jannis Kounellis (b. 1936)
To Be Invented Here and Now
(*Da inventare sul posto*), 1972
Oil on canvas, 247 × 300 cm
Score of "La Pulcinella" by Igor Stravinsky,
to be performed by a ballerina and a violinist
Collection of Dr. Rainer Speck, Cologne

The earliest attempts to find new forms of transcription, however, had been made by artists at the Bauhaus. In 1921–22, Paul Klee conceived a graphic representation of a three-part sonata movement by Bach. Kandinsky developed his "sound points" on the basis of Beethoven's *Fifth Symphony*.[69] Heinrich Neugeboren transposed a few bars from Bach's *Fugue* in E-flat minor into a diagram for a three-dimensional sculpture. And Peter Röhl in 1926 developed an interlinear score based on hearing a piece of music. Later, a number of artists such as Robert Strübin, Luigi Veronesi, or Jakob Weder concerned themselves with a systematic color–sound transcription intended to inspire composers to work out polychrome notations. A synthesis of painting, score and performance was demonstrated in Jannis Kounellis's 1972 project *To Be Invented Here and Now*, a piece which was to be "played in front of the image" and danced.

Takis (b. 1925)
Luminous Musical Telesculpture
(*Telesculpture musicale lumineuse*), 1966
Wood, electromagnet, needles, piano wire,
lamp, motor, 198 × 59 cm
Kunstmuseum Düsseldorf

Plastic Sound

The convergence of the two arts over the course
of the century can be roughly described as an increasing temporalization of painting, accompanied
by an increasing spatialization of music. "Through
the sheer transformation of the medium of time
per se into a material, as through the reduction of
what transpires in it into acoustic materials, a
spatialization emerges," noted Theodor Adorno in
1967.[70] The idea of what Werner Haftmann termed
a "musical space configuration" had admittedly
emerged much earlier, with Antheil, for instance,
who dreamed of urban orchestral machines whose
sounds would "shoot obliquely into space,"[71] or with
Varese, who spoke of "sounds as mobile tone-bodies
in space" and who envisaged a "spatial music" quite
akin to that which was later realized with the aid
of electronics and a distribution of sound sources
throughout a given space, by Stockhausen among
others.[72]

At this juncture, the sculptors applied their skills
to a unification of plastic volume and sound. What
the Futurists had already partially achieved with
their noise sculptures was taken up again and
systematically ramified in the 1950s.

One of the first sculptors active in the field was
Jean Tinguely, with motorized sound and noise
sculptures developed out of the spirit of the materials employed. His close affinities with music can
be traced all the way from his 1958 relief cycle *My
Stars—Concert for Seven Pictures* to the *Stravinsky
Fountain* in Paris, one of the finest urban multimedia works of the present day, created in collaboration with Niki de Saint-Phalle. Its interplay
of colorful figures and symbolic machines such
as a water-spouting treble clef evokes some of
Stravinsky's most popular compositions, such
as *Ragtime* or *The Firebird*.

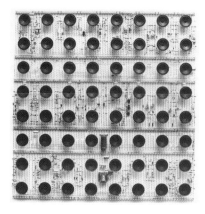

The spectrum of acoustic sculpture extends from the hypersensitively reacting sound-reliefs of a Pol Bury or Takis to the metallically clanging calyxes of the Baschet brothers, all the way to Meret Oppenheim's *Tune Towers*, which render the spatial dimension of acoustics perceptible through the various heights of its sound-generating tower structures.

The development of digital sound generation, which puts every conceivable tone of any color or volume at the fingertips of anyone who can deal with the technology involved, has made it possible to infinitely manipulate sound and employ it as a space-shaping medium. Bernhard Leitner, for instance, has developed "acoustic beds and cubes" which enable the user to experience sound not only in spatial but in physical terms, with one's entire body. Other artists, such as Giers or Vogel, program their sculptural configurations with combinations of electronic tones which are triggered by the viewer's movements, thus making him or her a participant in the work.

Walter Giers (b. 1937)
Music for 64 Loudspeakers
(*Musik für 64 Lautsprecher*), 1976
Electronic equipment, plexiglass
and 64 loudspeakers, 120 × 120 cm
Städtisches Museum, Schwäbisch-Gmünd

Jean Tinguely (1925–1991)/
Niki de Saint Phalle (b. 1930)
Stravinsky Fountain Paris, 1983
View by night

Opposite page, top:
Overall view of the fountain

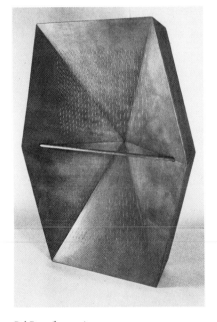

Pol Bury (b. 1922)
26 Strings and their Baton
(*26 cordes et leur bâton*), 1974
Acoustic sculpture, wood and strings,
160 × 120 × 58 cm
Galerie Maeght, Paris

The blurring of the borderlines between the sibling arts over the past decade and the emergence of new audiovisual hybrids has been demonstrated in a number of recent exhibitions, such as *Ars Electronica* in Linz, Austria, in 1989; *Klangräume—Raumklänge* in Kassel, Germany, in 1991; *Klingende Dinge* in Hanover, in 1994; or the Berlin Festival *Sonambiente*, in 1996. A highly diverse range of acoustic installations, soundscapes, video art, music environments, and performances has established itself, and draws freely on the latest media and technologies both visual and acoustic. Artists such as Stephan van Huene, Christina Kubisch, Rolf Julius, Max Neuhaus, Sarkis, Murray Schafer, or Yufen Qin have created in this interactive field works of the most diverse—if frequently only temporary—character. Others, such as the Dutchman Paul Panhuysen, do not use modern technology, but produce sounds using natural resources such as wind and water. The Hamburg artist Andreas Oldörp has even revived the idea of the pyrophone

and ramified it into highly complex sound–space installations. "Since the viewer has to establish his coordinates in this unfamiliar acoustic environment, he experiences his own real time and his subjective standpoint," explains Helga de la Motte. "Acoustic art enables experiments in consciousness. Being an experimental art, it has an open-ended character. Still, the advances in materials and technologies have made it into a genuinely unique, internally differentiated aesthetic field. It has established itself alongside the traditional genres as an art form in its own right."[73]

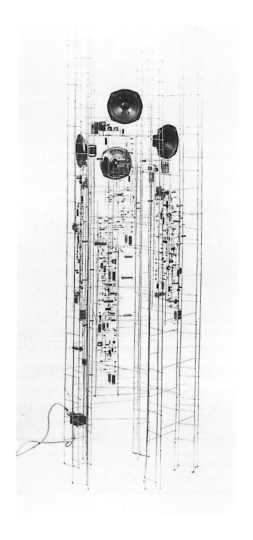

Above:
Andreas Öldörp (b. 1959)
From Space to Place
(*Vom Raum zum Ort*), 1998
Glass tubes, silver-plated copper, organ fan
Installation in the Galerie der Stadt Backnang
(six rooms)

Right:
Peter Vogel (b. 1937)
Minimal music piece for 7 players,
musical-kybernetic tower (Musikalisch-
kybernetischer Turm), 1983
Wire, photo-electric cells, resistors,
capacitors, loudspeakers, transformers,
165 × 48 × 41 cm
Staatsgalerie Stuttgart

Yufen Qin (b. 1954)
Spring in the Jade Hall, 1994
Laundry rack, clothespins, rice paper,
loudspeaker, electric cords
Installation in Rotunda Court,
Staatsgalerie Stuttgart, 1995
Photograph: Frank Kleinbach, Stuttgart

All of this would not have been possible without
the pioneers in the field, artist–composers active
since the 1960s—for example John Cage, La Monte
Young, Terry Fox, or Mauricio Kagel—for whom the
production of sounds and innovative instruments
increasingly took on the character of a sculpting
of space and time that lent a new dimension to
contemporary music in general. Just as in the visual
arts color has liberated itself from the picture
plane to expand into space and physically affect
the viewer, so music, whether instrumental or
electronically generated, has increasingly become
an unprecedentedly direct, physical experience.

1 Cf. Theodor W. Adorno, "Zum Verhältnis von Malerei und Musik heute" (c. 1950), in Th. W. Adorno, Gesammelte Schriften, vol. 18 (Frankfurt, 1984), pp. 143–44.

2 Wassily Kandinsky, Rückblicke (Berlin, 1913; 3rd edn., Bern, 1977), pp. 15 and 24.

3 Quoted in Eva-Maria Triska, "Die Quadratbilder Paul Klees," in Paul Klee—Das Werk der Jahre 1919–1923, exh. cat., (Kunsthalle Köln, Cologne, 1979), p. 78, note 80.

4 Quoted in Franzsepp Würtenberger, Malerei und Musik. Die Geschichte des Verhaltens zweier Künste zueinander (Frankfurt, Bern, and Las Vegas, 1979), p. 53.

5 Quoted in Jörg Träger, Philipp Otto Runge und seine Werke (Munich, 1975), p. 82.

6 Quoted in Hannah Hohl, Philipp Otto Runge, Die Zeiten – Morgen (Hamburger Kunsthalle, Hamburg, 1997), p. 22.

7 After the author's translation from Baudelaire, Curiosités esthétiques/L'Art romantique et autres Oeuvres critiques, ed. Henri Lemaitre (Paris, 1962), p. 696.

8 After the German translation by Erich Meyer (1898), quoted in Friedhelm Kemp and Hans T. Siepe (eds.), Französische Dichtung, Dritter Band, Von Baudelaire bis Valéry (Munich, 1990), p. 3.

9 After the author's translation of the original, quoted in Victor Segalen, Les Synesthésies et l'Ecole Symboliste, revised edn. by Eliane Fromentelli (Montpellier, 1981), p. 53.

10 Cf. Günter Metken, "Debussy und die Künstler des Fin de Siècle," in Karin von Maur (ed.), Vom Klang der Bilder (Munich, 1985), pp. 336–39.

11 Quoted in Kuno Mittelstädt (ed.), Paul Gauguin – Briefe und Selbstzeugnisse (Munich, 1970), p. 211f.

12 Gauguin, 1895; quoted in Pierre Schneider, Matisse (Munich, 1984), p. 308, note 73.

13 Ibid., note 69.

14 Ibid., p. 297.

15 Ibid.

16 Quoted in Walter Hess, Das Problem der Farbe in Selbstzeugnissen moderner Maler (Munich, 1953), p. 92.

17 Cf. Dorothee Eberlein, "Ciurlionis, Skrjabin und der osteuropäische Symbolismus," in von Maur (ed.), Vom Klang der Bilder, p. 345.

18 Cf. Gabriella Di Milia, "Mikolojus Konstantinas Ciurlionis," in 'Cahiers du Musée National d'Art Moderne,' no. 3, 1980, p. 59.

19 Quoted in M.K. Ciurlionis (exh. cat.) (Wallraf-Richartz-Museum, Cologne, 1998), p. 53.

20 Wassily Kandinsky, Rückblicke (Berlin, 1913; 3rd edn., Benteli, Bern, 1977), p. 14.

21 Wassily Kandinsky, Über das Geistige in der Kunst (1912; 4th edn., Bern, 1952), p. 64.

22 Ibid., p. 91f.

23 Quoted in Jelena Hahl-Koch (ed.), Arnold Schönberg – Wassily Kandinsky: Briefe, Bilder und Dokumente einer aussergewöhnlichen Begegnung (2nd edn., Munich, 1983), p. 178.

24 Letter of 14 January 1911, in Wolfgang Macke (ed.), August Macke – Franz Marc, Briefwechsel (Cologne, 1964), p. 40f.

25 Hahl-Koch (ed.), Arnold Schönberg – Wassily Kandinsky: Briefe, Bilder und Dokumente einer aussergewöhnlichen Begegnung, p. 19.

26 "Über das Geistige in der Kunst," quoted in Hahl-Koch (ed.), Arnold Schönberg – Wassily Kandinsky: Briefe, Bilder und Dokumente einer aussergewöhnlichen Begegnung, p. 42.

27 "Die Bilder," in Arnold Schönberg. Mit Beiträgen von Alban Berg, Paris von Gütersloh, K. Horwitz, Heinrich Jalowetz, W. Kandinsky, et al. (Munich, 1912), pp. 63 and 59.

28 "Über die künstlerischen Ausdrucksmittel und deren Verhältnis zu Natur und Bild," in Kunst für Alle, vol. XX, 1904, p. 132.

29 Cf. letter from Kandinsky to Schoenberg, 9 April 1911, in Hahl-Koch (ed.), Arnold Schönberg – Wassily Kandinsky. Briefe, Bilder und Dokumente einer aussergewöhnlichen Begegnung, Salzburg and Vienna, p. 25.

30 On this topic see H. Düchting, Robert Delaunays Fenêtres: peinture pure et simultané, Ph.D. dissertation, Munich, 1982, p. 468ff. On the issue of time in art, useful sources include H. Kern, "Zeit-Bilder. Zur Bedeutung von Bewegung in der Malerei des 20. Jahrhunderts," in Dimension IV, Neue Malerei in Deutschland, exh. cat. (Berlin, Munich, and Düsseldorf 1983–84), pp. 43–57; also the exhibition catalogues L'Art et le Temps, Regards sur la Quatrième Dimension (Geneva, 1985), and Raum-Zeit-Stille (Cologne, 1985).

31 Margaret Rowell, in Frank Kupka, exh. cat. (Zurich, 1976), p. 28.

32 M. Mladek, "Kupkas Weg zu Neuer Realität durch Musik" (English language manuscript, Washington, 1985); excerpts published under cat. 104.

33 Quoted after M. Mladek, in Frank Kupka (exh. cat.) (Cologne, 1981), p. 72.

34 Cf. Gail Levin, Synchromism and American Color Abstraction (New York, 1978), p. 129.

35 "Das Licht," in H. Düchting (ed.), Robert Delaunay, Zur Malerei der reinen Farbe. Schriften von 1912–1940 (Munich, 1983), p. 125.

36 Ibid.

37 Ibid., p. 138.

38 Ibid., p. 40.

39 Diary entry, July 1917, in Felix Klee (ed.), Tagebücher von Paul Klee 1898–1918 (Cologne, 1957), p. 380.

40 Apollinaire, in "Soirées à Paris," 15 June 1914. Quoted in M. Hoog (ed.),

Robert und Sonia Delaunay, collection cat. (Musée National d'Art Moderne, Paris, 1967), p. 132.

41 Rimbaud, "Fieberphasen II—Schwarzkunst des Wortes," in Sämtliche Dichtungen, trans. Walther Küchler (Hamburg, 1963), p. 227.

42 W. de Romilly and J. Laude, Braque: Cubisme 1907–1914 (Paris, 1982), p. 51.

43 P.E. Küppers, Der Kubismus, Ein künstlerisches Formproblem unserer Zeit (Leipzig, 1920), p. 40.

44 D.H. Kahnweiler, Juan Gris, Leben und Werk (Stuttgart, 1968), p. 148.

45 Cf. H. Kern, "Zeit-Bilder. Zur Bedeutung von Bewegung in der Malerei des 20. Jahrhunderts," in Dimension IV, Neue Malerei in Deutschland, exh. cat., p. 46f.

46 Cf. explanation by Luigi Russolo of the reproduction of his painting in the journal Poesia, December 1920.

47 Cf. P. Iden and R. Lauter (eds.), Bilder für Frankfurt, Bestandskatalog des Museums für Moderne Kunst (Munich, 1985), no. 125, p. 202.

48 A.E. Krutschonych, "Die ersten futuristischen Veranstaltungen der Welt" (1932), in Sieg über die Sonne, Aspekte russischer Kunst zu Beginn des 20. Jahrhunderts, exh. cat. (Akademie der Künste, Berlin, 1983), p. 51.

49 Quoted in Alla Powelichina, "Michail Matjuschin—Die Welt als organisches Ganzes," in Matjuschin und die Leningrader Avantgarde, exh. cat. (ZKM, Karlsruhe, 1991), p. 32.

50 Quoted in German Karginov, Rodtschenko, (Paris and Budapest, 1977), p. 193 [after author's German translation from the French].

51 J. Itten, Kunst der Farbe, Subjektives Erleben und objektives Erkennen als Wege zur Kunst (Ravensburg, 1961), p. 15.

52 "The intention was to contrast three movements with one another, much as in a symphony, whereby the blue, dark, would convey a quiet feeling, adagio, while the red with the round forms would engender the strong, clear movement, and the yellow window ... would give the impression of something extremely alive," was Hölzel's explanation of his Bahlsen windows. Quoted in W. Venzmer, Adolf Hölzel, Leben und Werk (Stuttgart, 1982), p. 126.

53 Cf. N. Troy, "Theo van Doesburg: From Music into Space," in 'Arts Magazine,' vol. LVI, no. 6, (February 1982), p. 93f.

54 Thomas Daniel Schlee and Dietrisch Kämper (eds.), Olivier Messiaen. La Cité céleste – Das himmlische Jerusalem. Über Leben und Werk des französischen Komponisten (Cologne, 1998), p. 167.

55 Olivier Messiaen, "Letzter Entwurf zu 'Conférence de Notre-Dame,' 4. Dezember 1977," in ibid., p. 169f.

56 On this subject, see especially the writings of A. Wellek, most recently

"Farbenmusik," in *Musikpsychologie und Musikästhetik*, Frankfurt, 1963, p. 166ff.; the more general discussion in F. Würtenberger, *Malerei und Musik, Die Geschichte des Verhaltens zweier Künste zueinander*, p. 191ff.; and the typescript dissertation by S. Selwood, *The Development from Abstract Art to Abstract Animated Film* (University of Essex, 1981). See also the essay by Selwood in von Maur (ed.), *Vom Klang der Bilder*, p. 414.

57 Cf. Marilyn S. Kushner, *Morgan Russell* (New York, 1990), p. 105ff.

58 Cf. *Stanton Macdonald-Wright*, exh. cat. (Washington, 1967), p. 23f.

59 Cf. note 54.

60 In this connection see also the exhibition catalogues *Electra* (Paris, 1983), p. 198ff., and *Klangkunst* (Akademie der Künste, Berlin, 1996).

61 Cf. Wolf Schön, in Günter Maas, *Klangbilder*, exh. cat., (Cologne, 1975), unpaginated (pp. 2–3).

62 Filippo Tomaso Marinetti, *Technical Manifesto of Futurist Literature*, 11 May 1912, in Umbro Apollonio (ed.), *Der Futurismus, Manifeste und Dokumente* (Cologne, 1972), p. 75

63 Vorticist manifesto quoted in von Maur (ed.), *Vom Klang der Bilder*, p. 130.

64 *Mondrian*, exh. cat. (New York, 1948). For detailed discussions of the effects of jazz on painting, see the essays by Karin von Maur and Gail Levin in *Vom Klang der Bilder*, pp. 368ff. and 400ff.

65 Cf. W. Hofmann, "Beziehungen zwischen Kunst und Malerei," in *Schönberg–Webern–Berg*, exh. cat. (Vienna, 1969), p. 110 ff.

66 Quoted in Noten, *Musikalische Schriftbilder und ihre Ausführung*, exh. cat. (Bern, 1974), unpaginated, p. 18.

67 On this topic, see also E. Karkoschka, *Das Schriftbild der neuen Musik* (Celle, 1996).

68 "Musik und Graphik" (1960), in *Texte zur elektronischen und instrumentalen Musik*, vol. 1, (Cologne 1963), p. 181.

69 Discussed in Kandinsky's essay *Punkt und Linie zu Fläche* (Munich, 1926; repr. Bern-Bumpliz, 1956) vol. 9, p. 44ff.

70 Theodor W. Adorno, "Über einige Relationen zwischen Musik und Malerei," lectures from the series "Grenzen und Konvergenzen der Künste" (Akademie der Künste, Berlin, 1965–66); published in *Schriftenreihe der Akademie* (Berlin, 1967), vol. 12, p. 9.

71 "Manifest der Musico-Mechanico" (1922), in *De Stijl*, vol. 6, no. 8 (1924), pp. 99–102.

72 Quoted in W. Haftmann, *Hommage à Schönberg*, exh. cat. (Nationalgalerie, Berlin, 1974), p. 36.

73 *Klangkunst*, exh. cat. published on the occasion of "Sonambiente – Festival für Hören und Sehen" (Akademie der Künste, Berlin, 1996), p. 17.

Albers, Josef 102–103

Balla, Giacomo 68, 73
Baranoff-Rossiné, Vladimir 82
Beuys, Joseph 108
Blanc-Gatti, Charles 88, 89
Boccioni, Umberto 71
Braque, Georges 60, 61, 62, 63
Brown, Earle 115
Bury, Pol 123
Bussotti, Sylvano 114

Cage, John 110, 111
Ciurlionis, Mikalojus Konstantinas 24–25, 26
Claudel, Camille 94

Dalí, Salvador 106
Delaunay, Robert 52, 54–55
Depero, Fortunato 72, 73
Doesburg, Theo van 84, 98, 99
Duchamp, Marcel 64, 110

Eggeling, Helmuth Viking 56–57, 58

Fantin-Latour, Jean Theodore 15

Gauguin, Paul 18
Giacometti, Augusto 27
Giers, Walter 122
Gris, Juan 66

Hartley, Marsden 44, 45
Hauer, Josef Matthias 83
Higgins, Dick 113
Hölzel, Adolf 39, 85

Itten, Johannes 40, 82

Javlensky, Alexei von 35
Johns, Jasper 95

Kandinsky, Wassily 28–29, 31
Klee, Paul 6, 8, 9, 13, 55, 117
Klein, Yves 112
Klimt, Gustav 17
Klinger, Max 16
Kounellis, Jannis 120
Kupka, František 42, 47, 50

László, Alexander 91
Lewis, Wyndham 97
Lissitzky, El 78

Maas, Günter 92
MacDonald-Wright, Stanton 49
Macke, August 34
Magritte, René 107
Man Ray 106
Marc, Franz 32, 33
Martinmüller, Armin 117
Matisse, Henri 21, 22, 23
Matyushin, Michail 80
Miró, Joan 74, 75
Mondrian, Piet 100, 101

Neugeboren, Heinrich 116

Ox, Jack 119

Paik, Nam June 109
Picabia, Francis 76
Picasso, Pablo 64, 65, 66–67
Puni, Ivan 79

Redon, Odilon 14
Richter, Hans 56, 57, 59
Roberts, William 96
Rodchenko, Alexander Michailovitch 81
Rühm, Gerhard 112
Runge, Philipp Otto 10, 11
Russell, Morgan 48
Russolo, Luigi 69, 70, 104

Saint Phalle, Niki de 122, 123
Schoenberg, Arnold 30, 36, 37
Schwind, Moritz von 2, 114
Schwitters, Kurt 104, 105
Severini, Gino 95
Skriabin, Alexander 90
Strübin, Robert 118
Survage, Leopold 92

Takis 121
Tinguely, Jean 122, 123

Valensi, Henri 86, 87
Veronesi, Luigi 119
Vyshnegradsky, Ivan 93

Weder, Jakob 118
Weissheimer, Wendelin 90
Whistler, James McNeill 16

Yufen Qin 125